How to Make America Utopia

Take away the economy from those who rigged it.

This page intentionally left blank.

Copyright & Contact

Copyright © 2021 by Egberto Willies.

Edited by Bruce Pollard.

Email: egberto@egbertowillies.com
Web: http://egbertowillies.com
Twitter: @egbertowillies

Table of Contents

Chapter 1: Introduction

There are times when I turn off all the lights in my studio and just meditate. I ask a whole lot of questions to the ethos.

- Why do most Americans continue to accept a system that moves so slowly in empowering one group after another?
- Why do Americans continue to support politicians who refuse to establish a health care system that takes care of all its citizens like every major industrialized country in the world?
- Why do Americans continue to support a criminal justice system unfair to people of color and all the poor even though their country preaches morality to the rest of the world?
- Why do Americans continue to tolerate an unequal educational system where public education is proportional to the wealth of the school district where one resides?
- Why do Americans accept a public college system that leaves most of the students with debt?
- Why do Americans give corporations the same rights we give human beings?
- Why do Americans allow politicians to spend more than the next 9 or so countries combined for a defense we will never need nor could we ever use?

- Why do Americans allow politicians to build toll roads, allowing private corporations to tax us for roads that should be built from taxpayer dollars?
- Why do Americans allow the working person's income to be taxed at a higher rate than investor income?
- Why do Americans allow corporations to use the patent system to stifle innovation?
- Why do Americans allow deregulation at the expense of their health and a clean environment?
- Why do Americans support an economic system biased to benefit the corporation and business over people?

The most important question of course is why did America, the country most grew up revering, fall from grace? Why did Americans elect the likes of Donald Trump?

A utopia is an imagined society that has perfect qualities for all its citizens. An American Utopia is a society where we create policies that give everyone equal access to success and happiness.

The reality

There are no satisfactory answers as to why Americans currently accept their plight. But there are reasons one can infer.

We have been indoctrinated and culturized from birth. That is not necessarily a bad thing.

I grew up in the church. I was indoctrinated with Christian values. Even as I have morphed into a Humanist, the values in which I was inculcated, remain a part of my most inner being. I have purged myself, as everyone should, of some of our most insidious practices, homophobia, and patriarchy.

Indoctrination is bad if it leads to an economy so flawed and unsustainable that it relegates most to eventual indentured servitude. It is bad if adhering to its tenets results in a society dependent on pitting communities and cultures against one another to ensure the supremacy of a few.

The angst in America is caused by the manufactured division between many identities, communities, and cultures. That angst becomes more and more necessary as our flawed economic system engulfs us like a dying star.

Keeping our defective economic system afloat requires people that do not understand how it works. Worse, it requires smoke and mirrors that hide and misrepresent its deficiencies.

We now have industries designed from their inception to lay the foundation necessary in our minds that set the parameters of debate and much more. The Powell Memo laid much of the current groundwork designed to mold Americans as droids of our economic system, as the puppets of the corporate masters.

Whenever a few people act outside of Powell's design parameters, the "system," the foundation planted in most of our psyche, ensures that we revert to form. Sometimes it is the state using coercion. Sometimes it is the state with the support of "we the people." And sometimes it is "we the people" acting organically.

Americans continue to revert to a permanent state of war because the state coerces them into believing that they are under permanent attack because of their freedom. War mongers use disjointed acts of terror, domestic and international, framed under a false narrative to prey on their fears.

The state, with the support of a subsection of the population, is complicit in reverting to a racist scapegoating past by making each immigrant, asylum seeker, and dreamer a persona non grata. Many quickly forget that the founders of this country were some of the first 'illegal aliens" on this land. The genesis of this country was enacted by people who came to conquer and take for themselves while those coming today just want a job.

Americans know that the current economic system is not working for them. By now many have already seen the charts that show a system where both income and wealth disparity continue to grow. Yet, when some propose alternatives that stops the pilfer by the few, there is pushback from a substantial segment within "we the people" who simply revert to the status quo. They are more comfortable reverting to form than exploring the alternatives.

Although we Americans view ourselves as exceptional, it turns out that we are just human beings like everyone else on the planet Earth. Fate has made us exceptionally rich and powerful because of geography, natural resources, and the continuous importation of intellect but we are like everyone else. When faced by the same forces, it turns out we all act the same. Yes, we are humans like all humans throughout the planet.

The modus operandi seen in countries where enough of the population accepts the terror from their country's respective plutocracy, is apparent in America. A faux educational system that allows indoctrination based on misinformation and disinformation continues to grow in America like it has around the world. Ours is just very polished. The chains are kept deep within our minds protected by a national façade.

Can we break out of our unsatisfactory and declining condition? Can we really become a utopian society? Can we make America our Utopia?

Of course, we can. But it requires engagement of everyone. It requires that we acknowledge our self-worth. Most importantly, it requires that we understand in the depths of our most inner-being that we are all equally worthy of our humanity and deserving of equal access to success.

America Held Hostage

When I re-engaged into an overt and immersive form of activism in 2010, I joined the Coffee Party USA, Move to Amend, and many other national organizations. One of the first pieces I wrote at Coffee Party USA was the following piece titled "Middle Class Held Hostage". The numbers have since gotten worse.

Middle-Class Held Hostage

Solving our nation's fiscal problems in a manner that is fair to every American requires honesty. It requires that we understand the real reasons for our budget deficits and not repeat the mistakes that got us here.

Our national debt is at $14.3 trillion dollars. Currently the average interest rate on that debt is about 3.2% which means before spending a penny this year on any government program, $460 Billion dollars from the American taxpayer will be transferred to the holders of our debt. Contrary to popular belief neither China (8%) nor the combination of all major countries in the world own most of our debts, Americans do.

President Reagan came into power in 1981 after convincing Americans that our debt was out of control inasmuch as at that time compared to this year's income, it was at a 50-year low. Republicans and Democrats alike voted for Reagan's budget that lowered tax rates substantially with the bulk going to America's most wealthy (trickledown economics). After Reagan's 8 years, the deficit was tripled. The deficit grew by another 55% under George H.W. Bush after he saw the light of fiscal responsibility and broke his no new taxes pledge. The budget was balanced under the latter year of the Clinton Administration and the debt was on a trajectory to decline. The budget doubled under President George W Bush after two tax cuts, again mostly to the wealthy, at the same time we were engaged in two wars.

America had its largest employment growth under President Clinton's administration and its poorest employment growth under President Bush. Trickledown (supply side) economics simply does not work, and most reputable economists will admit as much. It fails especially in times of globalization because tax cuts to the wealthy are likely not invested in America but in countries where growth rates are higher because of slave labor and a lower standard of living.

Over the last 30 years, we have dramatically reduced taxes mostly on the wealthy. This resulted in large deficits that all taxpayers are responsible for. Before a penny of taxes is used for entitlements, defense, and infrastructure, a disproportionate amount must first be transferred to mostly the wealthy owner of the debt. Notice they profit at both ends as they can keep more money from lower taxes and then purchase the US debt which pays them a good interest rate over time. That is the ultimate form of transferring wealth from the middle class to the rich.

Sadly, Republicans have decided to hold the middle-class hostage again. They want to lower the deficit solely by lowering spending. In other words, the real genesis of the budget deficits was caused by tax cuts and policies that benefitted the wealthy but the pain of closing the gap must be done on the backs of the middle-class. The rhetoric must not be believed.

While we must remove waste from our entitlement programs our real problem is that of too low a tax rate on higher incomes. When the top 1% gets more than 20% of the country's income and owns more than 40% of all of the country's wealth, there is a problem.

While it is true that 2% of Americans are responsible for a substantial portion of taxes and less than 60% of Americans pay federal income taxes (though they pay social security, Medicare, state, and other taxes) one must ask why. It is not that the top 2% is taxed too high; it is that they own most of the wealth and income. They do not own most of the wealth and income because they are more productive than the average middle-class American. They own the wealth because of a structural defect in our economy and how wealth grows, how wealth is earned, and how wealth is transferred. After all, the middle-class pays social security taxes on all their income while the wealthy do not. The working person pays up to 35% of their income in federal taxes while the investor pays only 15% on his capital gains.

> *The point is we created an economy that assigns worth arbitrarily and if one looks at one's value to society, those that control capital are the least valuable, yet they are the wealthiest. Yet, our teachers who are the foundation of our nation and the middle class must fight for their worth.*

The piece went viral on our networks. The leader of the organization asked that I write more of those pieces. Soon after I became a board member. It was clear we were at a tipping point in America.

America was ripe to really understand what was going on. The world's economy was on the verge of a collapse. People all over the world knew there was something wrong. The Occupy Wall Street movement in New York's Zuccotti Park exploded into existence in 2011 and spread throughout the U.S.

We thought we were at the brink of change. The Plutocracy and their puppets, (read "our government") were careful. They knew they had to crush the movement before it metastasized irreversibly. They played the semi-long game and ultimately were able to clear out all the Occupy

Wall Street encampments throughout the country.

You will hear many stories about the reason for the ultimate physical demise of the protest/movement. The best answer I found was the one we discussed in the organization Move to Amend.

The movement consisted mostly of middle-class and well-off, white, individuals. In other words, it did not have sufficient buy-in from all the aggrieved, poor, and middle-class alike.

In addition to being a movement that did not sufficiently represent the entire cross section of America, we simply were not ready. An effective representative democracy in my humble opinion can only be successful with an educated population. We must understand not only our rights but how our government functions in and out. More importantly, we must be educated about how our economy functions. dispelling the indoctrination of how the powers-that-be would like us to believe it functions.

In that light, many organizations like Move to Amend and Coffee Party USA, along with hundreds of small operations and organizations on meager budgets. have dedicated resources to inform and educate. Many of us believe that there is a certain homogeneity in wants when we are all playing from knowledge, from truthful verifiable information that ultimately gets down to our personal realities, feeding, educating, and keeping our families healthy.

So, while the Occupy Wall Street protests have subsided, and most of the subsequent protests have been either silenced or have voluntarily gone into hiatus, the processes of enlightening and informing our fellow Americans are gaining traction throughout the nation.

The goal of this book

The goal of "**How to Make America, Utopia**" is multifaceted. Our problems are not simple nor one-dimensional. We must connect the dots not sequentially but, in a network, to explain the economy and its interrelation with other societal issues.

Many people have a distorted view of their value to society. They look at folks like Jeff Bezos, Bill Gates, and Steve Jobs as geniuses, meritorious of the gargantuan wealth they have accumulated. This book will show that that wealth is not all theirs. It explains how the excess labor and intellect you voluntarily provided them was human capital they expropriated. Then they took advantage of what you produced to explode their personal wealth.

No one taught us that actuality in high school or college. That was by design. We cannot expect most people to implicitly know these concepts either. We have been programmed to believe that things can only work the way they work now. We are discouraged from taking a more informed look, a deeper dive, into what could be because it will disrupt the status quo; the one that favors a few and not the many.

This book will empower the masses to understand that they must assert their worth if they are to make an egalitarian society. Cheerleading and protesting without knowledge are not enough. One must understand all aspects of the system if we are to change it successfully.

This book is truthful. More importantly, it is practical. It exposes the misinformation that has been told for generations. It shows how the false basis of our economy is responsible for most Americans' inability to succeed independently or to get the services they need from the government.

This book heeds one important point. For Americans to buy into changes to a multitude of issues, they must first understand the causes for the present situation. They must see a vision, and have a genuine feeling that all the necessary changes in policies will lead to a cohesive and pleasurable existence as citizens.

How do we get there?

Is making an American Utopia all pie in the sky? Is it even possible to create an American Utopia? Of course, it is. But it will likely occur first by creeping, then walking, then running, and finally sprinting.

There are too many institutional structures within our society intent on maintaining the status quo. We must infiltrate them. We must change them where possible and eradicate them when necessary.

Changing our society will not be easy. We must work on two tracks.

The first track is ridding psyche of the fallacies that society taught us through indoctrination. As we re-educate the masses via independent media, rallies, and get-togethers, the political and social awareness of the masses will eventually burst into action.

The second track is morphing the educated masses into movements that will breed a new crop of Progressive elected officials. These new politicians will create the policies necessary for a more egalitarian society.

This process is already in effect with several young Progressives asserting themselves in

Congress. They are not afraid to challenge the status quo.

We must be frank. We must let people know up front that we will not transition into a better society overnight.

Making a more egalitarian America is not a one, two four, or eight-year effort. It is likely a twenty-five-year effort. Our society will improve progressively as we transition to our shared vision of a possible utopia.

The Plutocracy does not want you to aspire for a better future in the aggregate. They want you to believe that our economic system can only work the way it is now. The intent is to minimize our demands and expectations, making us participants in maintaining the status quo.

Chapter 2: About indoctrination

Creating a society requires a certain level of indoctrination of the masses. Indoctrination is not necessarily a bad thing if the outcome is satisfactory for those under its purview. It is however terrible if it ultimately results in a bias against some or disproportionate harm to others.

Unfortunately, often one is unaware that one is getting indoctrinated. And that is the whole idea. The best forms of indoctrination are ones done in a stealth manner. By the time the subject realizes what is happening, it is too late, and deprogramming is exceedingly difficult.

Over the last several decades, the American Plutocracy led a multifaceted indoctrination campaign on Americans. Unfortunately, the people capable of halting it never stood up or did not have the power to do so.

The seminal document with the path to said mind control was there for all to see, The Powell Memo aka The Powell Manifesto aka the Powell Memorandum. Upon deconstructing this document, one immediately understands the pathology afflicting a large percentage of Americans today.

Religious Indoctrination

Religious faith is a form of indoctrination. To be clear, one should have the utmost respect of every person's religion as long as the practice of one's faith does not impact another who has no desire to be impacted.

Religion demands that one accepts the edicts of a myth, scroll, or pass down story. It defines a hierarchy that one theoretically cannot, must not, and generally does not change. Because we are generally immersed in a doctrine it becomes second nature and accepted as fact; the way things are.

The plurality of Americans are Christians. The doctrines and practices of other religions seem strange to many of them. As a former Christian (now a Humanist), many times in my Christian days, I would look at the doctrines and practices of another religion with apprehension.

"How could they possibly believe that?" I would ask. "That does not make any sense."

I now realize how my thought process was completely hypocritical. A friend once made it clear to me.

"You are worshiping a god who you make seem to be so insecure that he wants you praising him all the time," the friend said. "He created everything perfectly, yet when his creation did what he did not want them to do, he burnt them in pain through eternity. But instead of simply using his power to absolve your sins, he sent his son to bleed and die a painful death to cleanse your sin. And by the way, he is invisible, you cannot hear him, but you think he speaks to every single person through their minds. Don't you think someone from another religion would find that strange?"

I am an engineer, a scientist. That statement gave me pause. At the time he told me that, I was already a Humanist as I recall. More importantly, it gave me humility and worked on my judgement.

Most religions are patriarchal. It is beyond the scope of this book to provide the rationale for that condition.

Even as society has liberalized laws, and we know for a fact that women are just as capable as men in every area, religious structures still sanction patriarchy. Most distressing is that this marginalization is applied with the consent of many women. That is a classic example of indoctrination.

Women are a <u>larger voting block than men</u>, especially in recent elections. They could elect more women and more Progressive politicians who support more women-centric policies. The fact that women voted for Donald Trump, basing their decision on religious doctrine, is probative of how effective indoctrination can be.

Patriarchal religions have justified many types of prejudice. They have justified slavery. They have perpetuated prejudice against gays, same-sex marriage and much more.

Many sects within religion have even jumped onto the economic bandwagon, as they attempt to morph capitalism into a tenet of Christianity. They promote it through a particularly crass religious ideology known as, *prosperity theology*.

Most distressing, however, is the church's unabashed entrance into the political domain. The alliance is dangerous. Why? The pseudo dictatorship, the *shepherd relationship* between the religious leaders and their pews, ensures that they can deliver to politicians for a price. And that is what they do.

Religion's support for Donald Trump and the current Republican Party shows the grotesque nature of said alliance. Indoctrination allows religious leaders to deliver winning votes even as those they support are anathema to past religious teachings and the Bible.

The alliance between the political sphere and religion is a clear and present danger. It must be eradicated.

Corporate Indoctrination

Did you know that corporations are legal persons with rights? Many corporations are large and awash in capital. As such they are superhumans. Their path to humanhood is complicated.

The documentary "<u>Legalize Democracy</u>" does a great job in explaining the path corporations took to gain the privileged status that rightfully belongs solely to flesh and blood human beings. Most importantly it points the way to real democracy not controlled by a corporatocracy.

How did we get here? Since the inception of the country, corporations have been attempting successfully to grow their influence and dominance in society. As Americans became more progressive, they began asking important questions. They started to demand what was rightfully theirs. They unionized, demanded equal rights, and much more.

The business class had to come up with a plan to temper the masses from realizing that they had been had over the decades by corporations. The U.S. Chamber of Commerce tasked Lewis Powell, a director at tobacco company Phillip Morris and a Ralph Nader dissenter, to write a confidential memorandum titled "Attack on the American Free Enterprise System," that was subsequently exposed by the Washington Post. The document was one designed to lay the blueprint to indoctrinate Americans into a pro-corporation stance. Lewis Powell, a Democrat, was subsequently appointed to the Supreme Court by Richard Nixon.

How did what would become known as the Powell Memorandum indoctrinate Americans into becoming either willful corporate slaves, or wards of the corporatocracy? The result infiltrated every aspect of our lives.

First, Powell defined the concerns of the Corporatocracy/Plutocracy as the momentum of mass movements was increasing.

> *What now concerns us is quite new in the history of America. We are not dealing with sporadic or isolated attacks from a relatively few extremists or even from the minority socialist cadre. Rather, the assault on the enterprise system is broadly based and consistently pursued. It is gaining momentum and converts. ...*

> *The most disquieting voices joining the chorus of criticism come from perfectly respectable elements of society: from the college campus, the pulpit, the media, the intellectual and literary journals, the arts*

and sciences, and from politicians. In most of these groups the movement against the system is participated in only by minorities. Yet, these often are the most articulate, the most vocal, the most prolific in their writing and speaking.

Moreover, much of the media-for varying motives and in varying degrees-either voluntarily accords unique publicity to these "attackers," or at least allows them to exploit the media for their purposes. This is especially true of television, which now plays such a predominant role in shaping the thinking, attitudes and emotions of our people.

One of the bewildering paradoxes of our time is the extent to which the enterprise system tolerates, if not participates in, its own destruction.

The campuses from which much of the criticism emanates are supported by (i) tax funds generated largely from American business, and (ii) contributions from capital funds controlled or generated by American business. The boards of trustees of our universities *overwhelmingly are composed of men and women who are leaders in the system.*

Most of the media, including the national TV systems, are owned and theoretically controlled by corporations which depend upon profits, and the enterprise system to survive.

Powell saw virtually every institution as the enemy of the Corporation. He describes the paranoia we see in the Republican Party, the Right Wing, and the neo-Liberal sect of the Democratic party.

He does not see the masses fighting for their piece of the pie as Democracy but instead an attack on corporate activities which many times are at best tantamount to the pilfering of the poor and middle-class, or worse, legalized theft.

In the memo, Powell accuses business of being too soft and aloof. His solution was a total infiltration in all parts of our lives. What exactly did that entail?

Infiltrate college campuses.

- *The Chamber should consider establishing a staff of highly qualified scholars in the* social sciences who do believe in the system.

- *There also should be a staff of speakers of the highest competency. These might include the scholars, and certainly those who speak for the Chamber would have to articulate the product of the scholars.*

- *In addition to full-time staff personnel, the Chamber should have a Speaker's Bureau which should include the ablest and most effective advocates from the top echelons of American business.*

- *The staff of scholars (or preferably a panel of independent scholars) should evaluate social science textbooks, especially in economics, political science and sociology. This should be a continuing program. ... We have seen the civil rights movement insist on re-writing many of the textbooks in our universities and schools. The labor unions likewise insist that textbooks be fair to the viewpoints of organized labor.*

- *The urging of the need for faculty balance upon university administrators and boards of trustees.*

Indoctrinate future business school graduates.

- *Should not the Chamber also request specific courses in such schools dealing with the entire scope of the problem addressed by this memorandum? This is now essential training for the executives of the future.*

Infiltrate Secondary Education.

- *While the first priority should be at the college level, the trends mentioned above are increasingly evidenced in the high schools. Action programs, tailored to the high schools and similar to those mentioned, should be considered. The implementation thereof could become a major program for local chambers of commerce, although the control and direction — especially the quality control — should be retained by the National Chamber.*

Indoctrinate the citizens at large.

- *Reaching the public generally may be more important for the shorter term. The first essential is to establish the staffs of eminent scholars, writers and speakers, who will do the thinking, the analysis, the writing and the speaking.*

Infiltrate the Media

- *The national television networks should be monitored in the same way that textbooks should be kept under constant surveillance. This applies not merely to so-called educational programs (such as "Selling of the Pentagon"), but to the daily "news analysis" which so often includes the most insidious type of criticism of the enterprise system.*

- *Effort should be made to see that the forum-type programs (the Today Show, Meet the Press, etc.) afford at least as much opportunity for supporters of the American system to participate as these programs do for those who attack it.*

- *Incentives might be devised to induce more "publishing" by independent scholars who do believe in the system. There should be a fairly steady flow of scholarly articles presented to a broad spectrum of magazines and periodicals — ranging from the popular magazines (Life, Look, Reader's Digest, etc.) to the more intellectual ones (Atlantic, Harper's,*

Saturday Review, New York, etc.) and to the various professional journals.

- *The newsstands — at airports, drugstores, and elsewhere — are filled with paperbacks and pamphlets advocating everything from revolution to erotic free love. One finds almost no attractive, well-written paperbacks or pamphlets on "our side."*

The memo urged corporations to spend 10% of their advertising budget to what one must define as public indoctrination. The memo also had marching orders for the stockholder. The corporation should be careful being outwardly political, leaving the heavy political lift partially to the shareholder.

If one doubts that complete calculated indoctrination favoring the corporation was the purpose of the memo, they should consider the following.

He wants direct political action as it indoctrinates the masses.

But one should not postpone more direct political action, while awaiting the gradual change in public opinion to be effected through education and information. Business must learn the lesson, long ago learned by labor and other self-interest groups. This is the lesson that political power is necessary; that such power must be assiduously (sic) cultivated, when necessary, it must be used aggressively and with determination — without embarrassment and without the reluctance which has been so characteristic of American business. As unwelcome as it may be to the Chamber, it should consider assuming a broader and more vigorous role in the political arena.

And of course, he wants control of the courts.

American business and the enterprise system have been affected as much by the courts as by the executive and legislative branches of government. Under our constitutional system, especially with an activist-minded Supreme Court, the judiciary may be the most important instrument for social, economic and political change.

The intent is clear, corporate control of the American mind. Even worse, politicians and the courts are enlisted to be the enforcers.

Scholastic Indoctrination

Scholastic Indoctrination is rather subtle and does not always have to be a bad thing.

Teaching a student about a good work ethic is a good thing for society. Enlisting political participation as a requirement to be considered a good citizen is a good thing. Learning the laws of the land, the reasons for them, and the consequences when we act outside their boundaries is important to society.

To some extent these are all American human-made tenets. They do not have to be as learned but we are taught to accept them. That is a form of indoctrination.

Another form of indoctrination is the lack of instilling these values in students but instead suggesting a contradicting "don't tread on me," individualistic, freedom that has little connection to the state or need for its services.

Americans now hear many politicians and scholars say, "Government is the problem." And many believe it. That is indoctrination and it is illogical. Government is "We the People." Are we implying we are bad? Government is us. Corporations can only control our every being if we first detach from ourselves, from our government, from "We the People."

Those are some of the values that the infiltration of the Powell Manifesto into schools have affected. Well aligned business schools and economic classes do not teach the values of different economic systems and how the best parts of them all can be stitched to create an egalitarian society.

We learn a false history that effectively dehumanizes all but a few. Did Christopher Columbus discover a land that was already there and populated? Were we really created as a representative democracy? How could that be when women and others could not vote.

There is so much we have been taught that is wrong, disingenuous, and outright false. Why is that? If Americans knew the truth about everything, change would be so much easier. The Plutocracy needs an ill-informed yet properly indoctrinated population. No one said that until our compass-less former president Trump pointed it out.

Media Indoctrination

Our evolving governmental system has designated the media as the fourth estate. It is the independent institution in our society with special rights. It is the media's responsibility to shine sunlight on everything, especially on the branches of our government to ensure they are acting as they should; we-the-people.

At times, the media behaves accordingly. It did its job exposing the corruption in the Nixon administration where Watergate led to his resignation. It followed the trail and exposed the Iran-Contra scandal where the United States illegally sold arms to Iran diverting some of the proceeds to support the Contras in Nicaragua. And of course, there was the Vietnam war reporting that ensured Americans would see what the war looked like as it exposed the lies of the administration.

Too many times, especially recently, much of the media has been either too lazy, too sympathetic to the Plutocracy, or outright derelict in its duty. It is not hard to find instances where these behaviors have cost the U.S. taxpayer trillions of dollars.

When George W. Bush was misleading Americans about the rationale for starting the war in Iraq,

Judith was the cheerleader at the New York Times. She was either snowed by the administration or willfully ignorant as she reported about the existence of weapons of mass destruction in Iraq. Her career was destroyed. She was forced to leave the New York Times in 2005. But by then the multi-trillion-dollar war was already in full force.

Then there were the lies about the Affordable Care Act that the media allowed to metastasize. Lying is not a difference in opinion on policy. The media in its fear to push back on what can only be described as one of its constituencies, allowed those opposed to Obamacare to appear on television with some of the most ridiculous lies imaginable. The media allowed the opponents to repeat the falsehoods ad nauseam. Sadly, the proponents of the bill were not savvy enough to combat the lies.

There were no death panels. There was no law equivalent to throwing grandma off the bus. It is impossible to have a government takeover of healthcare if private insurance companies are still in charge of paying the healthcare bills of most Americans. The media did not throw cold water on the lies. They did not ban the opponents from using the airwaves that belong to us for lying to the American people to affect a status quo outcome. For all practical purposes, they were remarkably successful. We did not get a single-payer Medicare for All system nor did we get a public option to compete with the parasites of capitalism, the health insurance companies.

And then there was the pseudo-marketing of Donald Trump. The media wanted their cake even as they ate it. They thought they could get tons of eyeballs by keeping the media-savvy former president on air without affecting the outcome of the elections. The media companies sold out the American people. They allowed Trump to come on the airwaves and say whatever he wanted to say. We all know the outcome.

The media continues to grant a platform to those who would mislead because news is just another profit center dependent on advertisers that neuters them forcing them to tow a certain line.

So, the fourth estate that is supposed to keep government and business in check is now propaganda engine. As such, we were misinformed on events leading up to the Venezuelan economic disaster, the war in Yemen, the Israeli-Palestinian conflict, the real motives behind the rightward turn of much of Europe, and much more.

Why does it work? Because many people still believe that if it appears on one of the network or cable channels it is real. That is Media Indoctrination.

Fortunately, as the methods of communicating with large audiences are democratized, the alternative media is getting stronger. The survival of our democracy depends on the balance alternative reporting has created.

We must be cognizant that with the slow demise of Net Neutrality, independent media could be in jeopardy. Rest assured, however, that people, dedicated to accurate reporting are working hard to force political change before any negative effects become permanent.

Chapter 3: The economic system explained objectively.

Too often, when people think about economics, they tend to think it is a complex subject better left to the experts. Do not feel that way. The basics of economics are remarkably simple. Economics is embedded within us. We have always traded and exchanged things.

The complexity within our current economic system is mainly a contrivance to empower a few. It is in the interest of those few to have people believe the economic system as we know it is divine and like the clergy are the emissaries of God, that their chosen few are the oracles of our financial health. As such, we cede our wants and needs solely to what they offer as plausible. But guess what? We can unmask that fallacy and take control!

The sole purpose of an economic structure is to create an infrastructure to exchange our products and services to enable a comfortable life.

It is not completely necessary to understand how our economic system came about over time. It is important to understand how it currently functions. This allows one to understand its deficiencies and to demand specific policies to fix it.

For all practical purposes, our economy is broken down into a public sector that is run by government and a private sector presumably run by individuals. That of course is an illusion that I will explain as we go over the different sectors of the economy.

The incestuous relationship between the government sector and a subset of the private sector will become evident. The negative consequences of that relationship will be in full view as you read various sub-sections.

Government Sector:

The government sector represents <u>approximately 21%</u> of the United States economy. While that is a large percentage, it is much smaller than the total size of the economy. The sector is primarily funded through taxes, fees, and bonds.

The government has three types of outlays. Mandatory spending like Social Security and Medicaid represents about 60% of the budget. Discretionary spending which includes the military budget and everything else is about 30%. Interest payments on the debt represent about 10%.

The government takes a lot of money out of the economy via taxes. It then spends it all into the national economy.

Let us immediately dispel an economic fallacy. When the wealthy seek tax cuts, they falsely claim lower taxes are magically better for the economy. An economy depends on the behavior of the people within it. As such, government spending is much more effective in economic activity than tax cuts.

I pointed this out in my previous book, "As I See It: Class Warfare the Only Resort to Right Wing Doom" where I wrote the following.

The basic tenet of supply side economics is that if you lower taxes on capital gains, other investments, as well as dramatically cut regulation on business that miraculously business will do the right thing to create products and services that people would want. Additionally, this philosophy distinctly supports unfettered free markets. In the process somehow tax revenues would increase to cover the loss revenue from the tax cuts.

As an engineer who believes solely in numbers, I remain baffled by academic institutions that allow this to be taught. The fallacy that increased taxes necessarily depresses an economy or that lower taxes automatically increase economic activity makes absolutely no sense. What matters in every case is how revenue is spent. If the expenditure is multiplicative increase economic activity occurs, period.

If the government increased taxes to purchase bread from Brazil to feed the poor in America that tax would demonstratively have a negative effect on our economy as all the additional employees hired and supplies purchased for the bread exported to our poor would create economic activity in Brazil while transferring the wealth of Americans overseas.

> *If the government increased taxes to help feed the poor in America by having more grain purchased from American farmers, more people hired to bake the bread, more ovens, mixers, and equipment purchased from American companies, a self-sustaining multiplicative economic effect occurs.*
>
> *Government simply lowering taxes does not guarantee that said savings would be reinvested into the economy. As such a marginal increase in economic activity cannot be guaranteed.*

Trump and his minions made many promises to get their 2017 tax cut scam passed. They promised that the tax give away would trickle down to the masses, it would ultimately reduce the debt by creating more economic activity, and that corporations would invest right back into the economy. Critics countered that corporations would simply do what they always do, buy back stocks to increase the stock price. That is exactly what they did. It blew up the deficit and transferred wealth to the rich.

The government spends virtually all the money it takes out of the economy via taxes and creates via debt. It can maintain stability if allowed to do so. The ability to do so is defined by Keynesian economics which we will not discuss in detail here [4].

Suffice it to say, the simple mechanism above illustrates the power and necessary role of government in the economy as a regulator. Unfortunately, some portions of the private sector have an inordinate control of the government which for selfish reasons prevents its smooth operation.

The tax cut scam perfectly illustrates the perils of allowing false narratives about tax cuts to take hold. A dollar does not know whether government or the private sector spends it. But an economy knows when that dollar is not spent it cannot circulate.

Private Sector:

The private sector is that portion of the economy that is owned by individuals. A pizza shop, a grocery store, a car rental business, a bakery. It is the largest portion of our economy.

When one thinks about the private sector, divide it into sub-sectors. One sub-sector controlled by large corporations with substantial political influence and the other sub-sector consisting of small businesses including mom and pop businesses. I consider the latter free enterprise companies and the former capitalist companies.

Many capitalist companies because of their political power and because they care solely about the bottom line at all costs are dangerous to democracy, the environment, and your health.

Free enterprise companies: the small restaurants, the small grocery stores, the small hardware stores, and others are slowly dying away as the capitalist companies use their political power and capital to destroy these businesses. Amazon, Walmart, and many other mega-companies without proper regulations from our government will destroy the fabric of a dynamic free enterprise economy.

Do not be fooled by the current low prices as these mega-corporations gobble up the small businesses. When the takeover is more complete, the capitalist companies, read: monopolies, will raise prices to whatever the market will bear. We cannot allow the takeover to continue unabated else our utopia will remain a wish.

Laissez faire is the order of the day in today's private sector. Virtually uncontrolled, it extracts profits without the wisdom of sustainability, humanity, or morality.

I appeared on a panel recently where we discussed the economy. The debate was about Donald Trump's tax cuts. A couple of us thought what we needed was a tax increase, mostly on the wealthy, by a substantial amount. Why? The excesses of the past several decades transferred the wealth of the middle-class directly to the relatively few who own capital.

There was a Conservative Republican on the panel. The first thing he asked was how was making the wealthy pay more going to affect business. He never asked how it would affect the wellbeing of the middle-class and the poor.

We pointed out that because the poor and the middle-class had more money, it would be great for the economy. After all, economic activity is measured by the velocity of money circulating.

The money of the wealthy sitting in a bank or in stocks is not circulating many times over throughout the economy. So, taxing the wealthy means more economic activity. It means the likelihood of more profit throughout. It is important to remember that being wealthy does not necessarily equate to logical thinking, just the opportunity to hoard at all costs.

He understood our argument but still felt better just holding on to all his money.

A strong and vibrant private sector is important, but it must have rules to prevent the accumulation of capital that stifles others from partaking of it.

Our current economic system cedes most of the power to private corporations. Their fiduciary responsibility is not to employees or customers but to the shareholders, the owners of these companies.

Laws are even on the books that prevent government from creating certain types of regulations. In fact, in some instances, corporations can sue the government for perceived lost profit if they deem a regulation hampers their business.

A well-regulated private sector lays out the playing field for everybody with an idea to innovate. A regulated private sector ensures a real meritocracy. In other words, one's access to wealth does not predetermine one's outcome.

It is for that reason that certain parts of the economy must be in the public sector with everyone having equal access, thus creating a level playing field that allows one to excel solely based on one's merit. How is this achieved?

- Everyone must have access to universal healthcare paid out of taxpayer dollars (Medicare for All).
- No one must be tethered to a dead-end job if they have an innovative idea.
- Everyone must have access to tuition-free college. They will clearly pay it back when they become taxpayers themselves.
- Everyone must have access to childcare. This means rearing kids does not inhibit employment possibilities.
- Everyone should be entitled to family leave. This ensures that family comes first.

Corporations do not like regulations. Why? They put everyone on a level playing field. The individual does not have to sell their labor at a discount. If business will not pay and they have an idea that is plausible, the chains the corporations use to hold on to employees are no longer there, healthcare, etc.

We must make the rules that govern humane happy living first. We can then fit the business model to support our humane society.

Applying these rules ensures that all businesses are on an even keel. As such no one business will have an unfair financial advantage over another.

Many will call this socialism. It is simply a humane model that works. It is not even novel as examples of this type of private/public sector alliances are found in the Scandinavian countries. And guess what, they are productive, and they are at the top of the happiness index.

Chapter 4: Billionaires, millionaires, and the wealthy class

Before we can make changes to the economic system, it is crucial to deconstruct the wealthy and discern if said wealth was earned or an aberration of a rigged system. There are legal means to mitigate unearned wealth.

There are two types of wealthy people. The first are those to whom wealth was given. The second are the ones who use the tenets of our economic system to develop wealth.

Inherited fortunes, lottery treasures and being chosen for venture capital are all forms of being given wealth. The same applies to executive bonuses and unwarranted salaries.

Is an executive who lays off workers and forces increased productivity from the remaining workers to maximize corporate profits really deserving of the bonus or should most of it go to the workers who made said profit a reality?

A startup team with an idea that captivates the American intelligentsia and gets huge influxes of capital from venture capitalists might ensure the idea is patented. Patenting freezes further development of that idea by others. The startup team's principals eventually get rich because they were the chosen.

When minerals are found on an owner's land, who should profit from those mineral deposits? That question is more profound than one may think. The natives in America, whose tribes were stewards of the entire continent, live in poverty and miserable conditions. Yet, those who took their lands, parceled it, and sold it, have created thousands of rich landowners.

The 2020 COVID-19 pandemic caused hundreds of thousands of mostly small businesses to close. Companies like Amazon & Walmart picked up the slack. In the process, the wealthy owners of these mega corporations got much richer. At whose expense did their fortune increase?

Texas did not want the Federal Government to regulate its electrical market, so they created their own distribution grid. The grid managers were warned for over a decade that they needed to weatherize their sources of electric generation. They forewent the advice to help their providers maximize their profits. When the severe 2021 expected freeze came, the Texas electric grid all but collapsed. In the process, the price of a megawatt of electricity went from around $20+ to over $10,000. That cost of course got passed to the consumer. For some it meant $20,000 bills for a few days of power. Many were overcharged because the power clearing house overpriced service for two days. The grid managers decided that since the power was being purchased off "the market" they would not attempt to unwind the overcharge. Now politicians want to bail out customers with federal taxpayer dollars. To be clear, the power companies and grid managers profited from not weatherizing their equipment and they profited from the disaster they created. Who paid? The middle-class taxpayer.

Our economic system is not designed to favor the deserving, but a select few. It is biased towards allowing those who reach a certain level of wealth to hoard it at the expense of everyone else.

The Jeff Bezos story clearly demonstrates the unfair balance of wealth in our country. We are led to believe that there is something exceptional about capitalist moguls like Bezos. Bezos did very well in school and college.

I encounter very smart intelligent people every day. In fact, the thought processes of many of my Politics Done Right listeners are downright genius. None of them will attain what Jeff Bezos has. Why? Mostly, because they have no interest in the headache or because they would be unlikely to get seeding capital for their dream.

Bezos received an Electrical Engineering and Computer Science degree from Princeton University. He worked for a couple of years for corporate America where he did very well.

Jeff Bezos then decided to form his own company, Amazon. This is where the mostly unknown story gets interesting.

Bezos received $300,000 in seed money from his parents to start his company. That was a lot of money at that time (1995). Most people simply do not have that opportunity. As such, a Bezos-like trajectory is impossible without taking advantage of someone. Even as Bezos was eating from his golden spoon, he was finding a way to maximize his money at the expense of others. How? He was considering opening the company on a reservation to avoid taxes.

The irony is that from an early age, the selfishness was palpable. It is exposed in the way Mr. Bezos hires and at the same time, how he delivers.

Having third party companies, indistinguishable from Amazon but with different responsibilities, pay scale, and liabilities delivers profit for Amazon. It is a deception that our economic system encourages.

How did Bezos get filthy rich? He became a parasite on steroids. He did nothing illegal. He just used an economic system that the public was indoctrinated to believe that being an effective parasite is superior and deserving of more wealth than anyone else.

Millions of people create products and services. Over time, Bezos used good thinking and his ability to get capital to create a monopoly to distribute products and services with a caveat. That caveat being; he got a substantial percentage of everything.

Do the 1.2 million employees partake of the spoils? The richest man in world limits their pay as he keeps the spoils which are equivalent to the GDP of many nations.

I wrote about another insidious way in which the Bezos of the world hurt us all in my book "As I See It: Class Warfare, The Only Resort to Right Wing Doom." I pointed out the following:

> *Amazon.com filed for a patent in 1997 on the procedure for placing an online order over the Internet. The procedure using the OneClick button used on the Amazon.com site was patented. This is tantamount to BestBuy patenting how a customer presents their credit card for payment for their products in some select way. The patent was ultimately granted. At the*

time I was contemplating creating a web-based ordering software package but because of the potential legal issues I may have to go through after investing substantial development time, I decided to scrap the project. This has probably occurred thousands of times. It inhibits healthy competition and total societal progress from the inability of having many different sources developing similar products and services which ultimate reduces cost and makes for better products and services.

I used Bezos as the poster boy of the failure and unfairness of our economic system. Here is the reality.

Our system teaches us as Americans, as westerners, that the wealthy like Jeff Bezos, are deserving of their accumulated wealth. They have worked hard, and that is the reason they are rich. Here is why that just is not the case.

Jeff Bezos had a great idea. He perfected selling books online and moved on to various other products, making Amazon what it is today. But is his concept worth him having $160+ billion of wealth? No, it is not. Even as many believe in the rewards of unfettered self-interest, it is false. This economic system, predicated on that fallacy, hurts most of its participants and is unsustainable over time.

Bezos' idea was neither unique nor implemented by himself. Moreover, Bezos' concept did not originate in his mind. The Internet, created by American tax dollars, the inception of online selling, and the technology wizardry of thousands of engineers and scientists made the idea possible.

An economic system is neither divine nor immutable. Our system is human made and designed to favor a few. We can transform it if we unshackle our mindset.

We must acknowledge our worth to society and strengthen our role in our economy. Human capital is more important and valuable than financial capital.

Movers of financial capital; bankers, stockbrokers, etc. are not more valuable than those who produce products and services useful to humanity, teachers, engineers, doctors, scientists, nurses, and many other professions.

The rules in our capitalist society support the idea that one can enrich themself by monetizing and not equitably sharing the spoils for an idea. The reality that one can enrich themself more than a products creator or the provider of services from the distribution of said products, is proof positive that our current economy is an immoral system.

The mathematically supported economic theory is that if a small percentage of people's wealth grows at a rate faster than that of the majority, then the system will collapse. Although it has not resulted in total failure, the present condition where people like Jeff Bezos and Bill Gates are accumulating wealth at a pace faster than the growth of the economy while most Americans are going through, stagnant wages and the inability to accumulate wealth validate the theory.

I covered a lot of these issues in my book "As I See It: Class Warfare the Only Resort to Right Wing Doom." Political economist and historian, Dr. Gar Alperovitz, covers solutions to several of these issues in his books "America Beyond Capitalism: Reclaiming Our Wealth, Our Liberty, and Our Democracy" and "The Next American Revolution: Beyond Corporate Capitalism & State Socialism." I interviewed Dr. Gar Alperovitz a few years ago when he laid out the migration from the undemocratic corporation to cooperatives and collectives where workers partake of the profits, they created instead of the spoils going to the few as unearned income.

Recent statements from several billionaires make it clear that these guys live in a different reality. When any of them gets a conscience, others seem to reel them in quickly.

Late in our 116th congress, Senator Bernie Sanders (D-VT) introduced a new estate tax bill called the *For The 99.8% Act (S309)*. The bill, in direct opposition to an earlier bill introduced by Senator John Thune (R-SD), called for a stronger and more graduated estate tax, with a top tax rate of 77% on estates over $1 billion. Clearly, one side of the aisle is listening to what the American people want, while the other side of the aisle is still listening to their donor class. Now, America's billionaire class needs to pick a side.

In response to the bill, Morris Pearl, former managing director at BlackRock, Inc., and Chair of the Patriotic Millionaires issued a statement in short order.

> *"Rather than being content with the enormous slice of pie they have already been given, America's billionaires are trying to keep the entire pie for themselves and their offspring. Their gluttony - and the political manipulation they employ to feed it - is ripping our country apart. Voters tried to change that at the ballot box. If that doesn't work, they are going to stop putting up with the billionaires altogether and do something*

more drastic. That is going to end poorly for billionaires who have been enjoying the good life, and for most of the rest of us as well.

We call ourselves the Patriotic Millionaires for a reason - because our country is more important to us than our money. The question is do any of America's billionaires care more about the nation than their pocketbooks. If they do, they will support this legislation."

This legislation would have lowered the current exemption to $3.5 million of an individual's estate, impacting only the wealthiest 0.2% of Americans. It would have also introduced a progressive, marginal tax rate structure to the estate tax, with the highest tax rate being 77% of the value of estates over $1 billion. In addition, the bill would have close loopholes in the estate and gift tax, including the ability to claim the value of an inherited asset is lower for estate tax purposes than what is claimed for income tax purposes. Protections for family farms was also included, as the bill allowed family farmers to lower the value of their farmland by up to $3 million for estate tax purposes.

Could it be that some millionaires & billionaires are starting to see the writing on the wall?

We must rid ourselves of the indoctrination we have been under since this country's inception. The indoctrination that was fortified by the Powell Memo. We need progressive mobilization to take hold as Americans start understanding how the corporate state was taking advantage of them. If we fail to do that, then welcome to indentured servitude.

No one on the planet is deserving of accumulating billions or even several tens of millions. Figuring out the cutoff point of wealth accumulation is above my pay grade.

The bottom line is this. The spoils should belong to those who create and make value. We all build on the knowledge, works, and service of millions of people that preceded us or are among us. That we have a system that denies the equitable distribution is an economic system that sanctions an esoteric form of thievery.

Chapter 5: Religion corrupts policy

A mature nation must make compartmentalization its modus operandi. Most social and religious issues tend to affect policies beyond their scope.

I have wondered for a long time how otherwise good citizens could get so hateful or heartless towards a fellow citizen. After all, most Americans are Christians and Jesus preached love, right?

I remember back when I was in college marching to force my University of Texas to divest its funds from South Africa. I went to the pastor of my church and I asked him to encourage the congregation to march with us. He said he would not support it.

I got mad at him and challenged him. After a lengthy discussion he pointed out that Jesus never spoke out against slavery and in fact he quoted Ephesians 6:5 "Slaves, obey your earthly masters with respect and fear, and with sincerity of heart, just as you would obey Christ." Suffice it to say I became a Humanist going forward.

Even though that one verse had a negative effect on me, the good values instilled in me from my Christian upbringing remained. In Panama, all our preachers were loving people and believed, in fact, that we were our brothers' keepers.

When there were conflicts, they took the position of agreeing to disagree. They would tell each other, "we must pray on it and God will eventually provide an answer." Church was the place everyone came for comfort.

Fast forward to today. The church, specifically the evangelical church, has become a political force with political power affected by an indoctrinated congregation. Church leaders have used their power to scare politicians into towing the lines on issues. They have used that power to deny rights to those they disagree with (e.g., gays) and policies they disagree with (e.g., birth control rights).

Most dangerous of all, they have allowed themselves to be coopted by the unfettered capitalist wing of the Republican Party. In doing so, they have formed an unholy alliance with those that support policies diametrically opposed to all that they used to stand for and that Jesus stood for.

Evangelical Christians came out squarely against healthcare reform that seeks to insure all Americans. They came out against a strong social safety net. A few years ago, Pastor David Hope in the article "Jesus is not a socialist" wrote in the Kingwood Observer:

Capitalism is like the kingdom of God. Everyone has an opportunity to make it to the top, but there will not be equal outcomes. When government tries to manufacture equal outcomes, it brings everyone down. As people concentrate on the sizes of the pieces of the pie, the pie just keeps getting smaller. All the pieces get smaller and equal outcomes are still not achieved.

This cannot be achieved as God has put into man the desire to succeed, because God wants us to succeed and prosper.

"Beloved, I wish above all things that thou mayest prosper and be in health, even as thy soul prospereth." 3 John 2

"This book of the law shall not depart out of thy mouth; but thou shalt meditate therein day and night, that thou mayest observe to do according to all that is written therein: for then thou shalt make thy way prosperous, and then thou shalt have good success." Joshua 1:8

Capitalism is the most compassionate system. Capitalism is the best way to reduce poverty. It gives every man a chance to succeed, and it promotes wealth into the hands of those who serve others and have a heart to give to those less fortunate.

> *It increases individual wealth, thus allowing individuals to give out of their increase. God has designed the needs of the poor to be met by Christians, not by the government. Government's bureaucratic shuffling of wealth accomplishes nothing.*

The pastor missed the point. Capitalism is a tool. Capitalism does not know humanity nor should it. We as humans make laws. If we are moral, we will make laws that benefit humanity first. We do not wait to enrich a few with the expectation that the rich would be benevolent to care for the poor. We make a system that gives all equal access. We do not allow a system that virtually enslaves for the benefit of a few. We do not create a system where those who simply shuffle money and capital but produce no product or service are deemed more worthy than all the rest. Work and deeds are what we reward.

Ultimately, I got it. Not having been in any of these churches in a long time, I did not notice the shift in tonality.

Many citizens look up to their pastor for leadership and direction. They believe these are men with knowledge and a direct link to what God expects of us. Messages of hate and prejudice by pastors in leadership provide the justification of parallel behavior by the congregations at rallies and other venues where a decidedly politicized and less than loving display is often evident.

I have told many of my Republican listeners to my show Politics Done Right that it is time to take back their party and make it stand for what it stood; conservative values without the loss of humanity. Christians, take back your church from the unholy alliance that it currently has with all those who are diametrically opposed to your true doctrine.

Passage of the Affordable Care Act is a perfect example that shows how religious doctrine is used as a pretext to neuter policies that help millions. The Hobby Lobby challenge to the Affordable Care Act is the perfect example.

In 2014 the Supreme Court ruled in a 5-to-4 decision that requiring family-owned corporations to pay insurance coverage for contraception under the ACA violated a federal law protecting religious freedom.

The two corporations, Hobby Lobby & Conestoga Wood Specialties challenged the ACA. The owners said they try to run their businesses on religious principles. The ACA and related regulations require many employers to provide female workers with comprehensive insurance coverage for a variety of methods of contraception. The companies objected about many of the methods, saying they are tantamount to abortion because they can prevent embryos from implanting in the womb. They said that providing insurance coverage for those forms of contraception would make them complicit in the practice.

Owners who purport to be pro-life, in their tunnel vision or willful ignorance, are unable to extrapolate what their decision really means. They are potentially sacrificing an inviable zygote for the health and possibly the life of their female employees. Who gives them that right? Do you think if it affected men, they would want the restrictions? Of course not.

This a perfect example why healthcare does not belong in the hodgepodge of the private sector. Therefore, religion has no place in governmental policy.

Chapter 6: Capitalism, socialism, fascism, communism

There must be a better way between the rails of today's ill-defined economic model. If the current model cannot sustain those subjected to it continuously, then it has failed. The model must be guided by humanity first with the ability to adapt in real time.

Webster defines the following economic/political models as follows:

capitalism:

An economic system characterized by private or corporate ownership of capital goods, by investments that are determined by private decision, and by prices, production, and the distribution of goods that are determined mainly by competition in a free market

socialism:

(1) any of various economic and political theories advocating collective or governmental ownership and administration of the means of production and distribution of goods

(2a) a system of society or group living in which there is no private property

(2b) a system or condition of society in which the means of production are owned and controlled by the state

(3) a stage of society in Marxist theory transitional between capitalism and communism and distinguished by unequal distribution of goods and pay according to work done

fascism:

(1) a political philosophy, movement, or regime (such as that of the Fascisti) that exalts nation and often race above the individual and that stands for a centralized autocratic government headed by a dictatorial leader, severe economic and social regimentation, and forcible suppression of opposition

(2) a tendency toward or actual exercise of strong autocratic or dictatorial control

communism:

(1a) a system in which goods are owned in common and are available to all as needed

(1b) a theory advocating elimination of private property

(2a) a doctrine based on revolutionary Marxian socialism and Marxism-Leninism that was the official ideology of the U.S.S.R.

(2b) a totalitarian system of government in which a single authoritarian party controls state-owned means of production

(2c) a final stage of society in Marxist theory in which the state has withered away and economic goods are distributed equitably

(2d) communist systems collectively

Forget about the capitalism vs socialism discussion in the United States. They are just buzzwords and scare tactics among most who do not have a clue about either political or economic system.

There is no democracy in our form of Capitalism

Understand that there is nothing democratic about capitalism or fascism inherently. Note that in Merriam-Webster's definition of capitalism, it seems benign and free. Neither is the word government nor political used. That is not true for their definition of socialism, fascism or communism. This is by design. Our dictionaries and books, have a bias designed to indoctrinate (read Powell Memo effect).

Here is a reality we have been living, especially since Ronald Reagan; unfettered capitalism decays into fascism. A study by political scientists Martin Gilens of Princeton and Benjamin Page of Northwestern illustrates that in fact the building blocks to fascism are in full vogue as the irrelevancy of the masses is increasing. They wrote the following[4].

> *Each of four theoretical traditions in the study of American politics—which can be characterized as theories of Majoritarian Electoral Democracy, Economic-Elite Domination, and two types of interest-group pluralism, Majoritarian Pluralism and Biased Pluralism—offers different predictions about which sets of actors have how much influence over public policy: average citizens; economic elites;*

and organized interest groups, mass-based or business-oriented.

A great deal of empirical research speaks to the policy influence of one or another set of actors, but until recently it has not been possible to test these contrasting theoretical predictions against each other within a single statistical model. We report on an effort to do so, using a unique data set that includes measures of the key variables for 1,779 policy issues.

Multivariate analysis indicates that economic elites and organized groups representing business interests have substantial independent impacts on U.S. government policy, while average citizens and mass-based interest groups have little or no independent influence. The results provide substantial support for theories of Economic-Elite Domination and for theories of Biased Pluralism, but not for theories of Majoritarian Electoral Democracy or Majoritarian Pluralism.

When the corporation buys politicians, these politicians' sole existence changes to serve the corporations and the wealthy elite. That means the politicians become unresponsive to the people who elected them. Again, unfettered capitalism above and beyond creating an immoral income inequality & wealth disparity decays into fascism.

If Americans understood the real reasons the middle-class is dying, our economic system would have been changed a long time ago. As the pain grows, it will become more evident.

The evidence will not come from our media. They will continue to allow the plutocrats to use our airwaves to mislead us about the real causes of our problems.

Capitalism serves shareholders, not you.

In its purest form, capitalism is an economic system whose sole intent is to serve the shareholder, above all. Economist Milton Friedman, one of the most followed evangelists of capitalism, wrote a New York Times op-ed a few decades ago that while not shocking to those missing a moral compass, will seem matter of fact for the heartless. He wrote the following:

> *WHEN I hear businessmen speak eloquently about the "social responsibilities of business in a free-enterprise system," I am reminded of the wonderful line about the Frenchman who discovered at, the age of 70 that he had been speaking prose all his life. The businessmen believe that they are defending free enterprise when they declaim that business is not concerned "merely" with profit but also with promoting desirable "social" ends; that business has a "social conscience" and takes seriously its responsibilities for providing employment, eliminating discrimination, avoiding pollution and whatever else may be the catchwords of the contemporary crop of reformers. In fact they are—or would be if they or any one else took them seriously— preaching pure and unadulterated socialism. Businessmen who talk this way are unwitting puppets of the intellectual*

forces that have been undermining the basis of a free society these past decades.

The discussions of the "social responsibilities of business" are notable for their analytical looseness and lack of rigor. What does it mean to say that "business" has responsibilities? Only people can have responsibilities. A corporation is an artificial person and, in this sense, may have artificial responsibilities, but "business" as a whole cannot be said to have responsibilities, even in this vague sense. The first step toward clarity in examining the doctrine of the social responsibility of business is to ask precisely what it implies for whom.

Presumably, the individuals who are to be responsible are businessmen, which means individual proprietors or corporate executives. Most of the discussion of social responsibility is directed at corporations, so in what follows I shall mostly neglect the individual proprietor and speak of corporate executives.

IN a free-enterprise, private-property system, a corporate executive is an employee of the owners of the business. He has direct responsibility to his employers. That responsibility is to conduct the business in accordance with their desires, which generally will be to make as much money as possible while conforming to the basic rules of the society, both those embodied in law and those embodied in ethical custom.

Understand what this passage means. If your sole goal is to maximize profits and growth, at some point the executive, who according to Economist Milton Friedman, is but an employee of the shareholders, must do what is necessary to fulfill that goal. And if the current societal ethics and policies are in the way, then the employee must do what it takes to change those. How is that done? By purchasing politicians to change the playing field; the policies to allow that profit maximization.

I believe in having an economic system that works for everyone. It must be democratic. The best system is a hybrid, free enterprise, with a robust safety net It should be a system unable to hoard capital which is a detriment to the economy.

Everyone should have the ability to create their companies if they so desire using their intellect and labor or work for others and get compensated commensurate with their efforts. Many who read some of my <u>anti-corporate/anti-capitalist well-researched rants</u> ,falsely believe that I am some blowhard who wants some socialist state where the takers abuse the makers. That is not so. What is clear is that the food stamp con artists share much in common with most of the unfettered capitalists. They are takers by design. They both profit from the labor and intellect of others (e.g., taxpayers, employees).

Too many people are resistant to change because they believe that our economic system is divine. It is not. It is "man-made," and it has all the features in it to ensure only the chosen can succeed. The Plutocrats used the tenets of the Powell Manifesto to brainwash many into believing that those who work the least, as long as they wear a suit and are in an "acceptable" economic space, are worthy of their income, wealth, and riches. That indoctrination has caused us to disparage the ever-growing discards of a failing system blaming them unfairly for the failures of our economic model.

The titans of commerce have made capitalism an ideology instead of a tool. As such its inhumanity and barbaric intrinsic nature are on full display for those who choose to see it. Adherence to this economic system requires an uncanny ability to make excuses for the reality that very few Americans have partaken of the country's growing wealth.

Many people point out that under our economic system we built great skyscrapers, monuments, and more. One must ask, what percentage of the population can take advantage or partake of the spoils. Most buildings, structures, and the like are off-limits for most Americans, yet we praise their existence as some collective accomplishment. They are not. Like slaves, workers built them for the benefit of a few other workers who are generally allowed entry just to serve. And that is the better side for most.

One must not forget the likes of the <u>Toys "R" Us saga</u>. Its demise can be directly attributed to vultures that shuffled a few papers to extract capital from the company in exchange for saddled debt. 30,000 unemployed American citizens were the waste, the byproduct of a few amassing an inordinate amount of wealth from the transaction making humanity irrelevant.

A few years ago, an Elon Musk <u>tweet showed</u> the ease with which, in his case, Tesla stock, but in the aggregate, the entire economic system can be compromised and/or manipulated. It is clear the emperor has no clothes.

Elon Musk Tweet: "Am considering taking Tesla private at $420. Funding secured."

Elon Musk's tweet and the resulting financial results should dispel any notion that the stock market, the life blood of our economic structure, is anything but a legalized, rigged, gambling platform. Nothing changed at the company to justify the change in the value of the stock, assuming it was based on anything other than a whim. Yet a tweet lost a lot of wealth for many and it made a lot for others. That is the definition of gambling; losing or winning cash without producing anything.

Many vultures shorted Tesla stock. Elon Musk's one tweet cost them $1.3 billion in just a few hours. Those guys produced nothing as they made millions on the service and innovation of others. Elon Musk turned the table on them yesterday as he pulled the rug from under them. Many think it is a bluff. But if it is not, the vultures would have justifiably lost their shirt as the price of the stock approached the supposed purchase price to take Tesla private.

Tesla has the type of problems any innovative cutting-edge company has and as such should not be judged on a quarter-by-quarter basis. Of course, do not tell that to the titans of finance who scrutinize the company ad nauseam. When companies enter a stage where the stock price may fall because of market forces or investor shortsightedness, financial vultures would enter and short the stock. Shorting a stock is an evil technique to profit when a stock falls in price.

Most financial companies make money not by investing in companies for the purpose of making money from the success of their products and services, but for merely by moving paper and money around. Their investments produce nothing useful for society. They generate money off the backs of others having formed companies, and others who have created products and services. I fail to see how this is substantially different from crooked welfare recipients. Maybe crooked welfare recipients should put on suits and ties as they use the system to get something for nothing. Oops -- corporate welfare recipients already do that, and it works. Working class welfare recipients: Are you listening?

To be clear, most citizens on welfare are there because they do not participate in an economic system that rewards the real value of work. We reward capital more so than human labor. In other words, those with capital, profit more than those who do the job to maintain that capital.

Our indoctrination has taught us that those with capital are more valuable to society. Put a farmer on a deserted island alongside a stockbroker. If each is left to their own device, who do you think would survive? Who is more valuable? The one with capital or the one who can produce something?

It is said that <u>capitalism affords the efficient allocation of resources</u>. That may be the case in theory. The reality is that it has failed to do that as it has allocated resources to the least deserving internally. For the economic system in the aggregate, it has allocated resources stupidly. Why are we burning fossil fuels when the technology exists to go green en masse? Why are the most productive workers paid less than paper pushers? One could go on and on.

Only when Americans understand the corrosive nature of the internals of our economy, will they force a change. When they realize that the economic system is not divine, but human-made will they engage to change the parameters to fix it in a manner that gives all equal access to success.

Progressives are scared to call out Capitalism by name just as they stare into the lights when the GOP calls them Socialists.

Again, when one looks up a definition of socialism, communism, and capitalism, the results frequently attempt to make communism and socialism similar. They are not. What grabbed my eyes was the following from Investopedia:

> ***"Both are the opposite of capitalism, where limitations don't exist, and***

reward comes to those who go beyond the minimum. In capitalist societies, owners are allowed to keep the excess production they earn. And competition occurs naturally, which fosters advancement. Capitalism tends to create a sharp divide between the wealthiest citizens and the poorest, however, with the wealthiest owning the majority of the nation's resources."

How difficult is it to turn *"owners are allowed to keep the excess production they earn."* into the phrases "stealing from," "pilfer of the worker," "moocher," "taker," or similar pejorative? After all, the Plutocrats, the capitalists, are enriching themselves from the intellect and labor of others. Ironically, as they take their unearned spoils, many of their employees are working several jobs to keep up, or they are on food stamps. This truth is not rocket science. It is the same pathology that keeps many majorities from improving at the behest of immoral minorities (read South Africa).

Here is a sad reality. I want to reiterate. Like the food stamp con artists who share much in common with most of the unfettered capitalists, they both make money off the labor and intellect of others. They both work out schemes in which they benefit financially on the backs of others. They both produce nothing to move society forward.

I know many will take exception. After all, didn't Bill Gates and Steve Jobs' intellect create mega computers that revolutionized efficiency and productivity? That is what you were taught to believe. Bill Gates and Steve Jobs were good at what they did. But most importantly, they were chosen. And then their monopolies froze most other entrepreneurs out of these markets.

Does anyone believe that only a few dozen Americans have the intellect and insight to do what they did? Just like thousands of churches have singers as good or better than Mariah Carey but not chosen; the same applies to technology. The American meritocracy is a fantasy. Merit is only a diploma that may get you to the crack of the door.

The GOP does an outstanding job at turning words used by Progressives into pejoratives. Progressives must do the same with their words. Interestingly, we would not have to use Cuba or Venezuela to prove the failure of the economic system. We need only ask them to look at their employee check, bank account, and credit card bills over time. Then look at the wealth of the

Plutocrat who watches them work. Do you feel worthy and meritorious now?

Corporate pricing power makes us powerless.

There is a basic tenet we must recognize in our economic system. Pricing of any product in our economic system has its basis on a corrosive concept known as "Whatever the market will bear." And what will the market bear? The market will bear all your income plus your total creditworthiness, plus how much you can borrow.

Sadly, the reality is that corporate officer whose fiduciary responsibility is to their shareholders and their huge undeserved salaries will keep raising prices until people are simply unable to afford what they are selling. If it is something people must have, Americans will spend up to their limit to get it.

The tenets of the current economic system are predicated on this behavior that effectively prevents us from saving. It makes us entities that are nothing, but conduits of our income, used to create the increasing wealth for a few; those who determine prices, the Plutocrats.

Ultimately, those with unregulated and unlimited pricing power on products and services you must have, can ensure you can never accumulate wealth. They own you. They can extort you.

As many small businesses had to remain closed to prevent the spread of COVID-19, Amazon, Walmart, and a few others made a killing. As the economy came back, the oil cartel raised prices. They did not care that many people driving back to work were already strapped. But in greed, they exercised their pricing power.

The above reality defines our economy, an odious form of capitalism. The proof is a continual decline in the wealth of the masses as the few get a more significant percentage. Unchanged, math prevails. Welcome to indentured servitude.

Chapter 7: The meritocracy fallacy; you are invited or chosen.

Many believe we live in a meritocracy. In my previous book, "It's Worth It: How to Talk To Your Right-Wing Relatives, Friends, and Neighbors," I touched on merit and the chosen in two chapters that is apropos.

In the chapter *"We must take back our wealth from the super-rich methodically before it is too late,"* where I included a speech by Mr. Gekko in the Wall Street movie that encapsulated the essence of Capitalism in the form we practice. I wrote the following:

> *I learned about free enterprise but was never indoctrinated by what our business schools try to impart on their students. Capitalism is not free enterprise, and Gekko was not an unrealistic character. We have come to see that today's plutocrats create more damage to the world economy than he ever could. They made an extractive, immoral, pilfering system acceptable.*
>
> *While still going through the process of learning the real economic system beyond the macroeconomics courses I took, I went

to see the Eddie Murphy movie "Trading Places." While the movie "Wall Street" was confirming, "Trading Places" was the movie that opened my eyes to the fraud of a system where those who produce with their labor and intellect were not the beneficiaries of their worth.

Eddie Murphy's character was a bum on the streets. Two plutocrat brothers made a bet that they could turn an executive into a bum, and a bum into a Wall Street executive. The experiment was successful for the brother who turned Eddie Murphy, the bum, into a stock trading executive.

The movie had a socioeconomic message. But most importantly, it showed how detached the capital markets are from reality. Even though it was just a movie, research shows there is little knowledge of anything substantive needed to be a player in the capital markets. One just needs to be chosen to be a member of the club, and being a member affords one an inordinate amount of control over the lives of millions, thanks to our corporate structure.

> *The plutocrat brothers in the movie bet one dollar on the experiment and would have destroyed two lives in the process had Eddie Murphy's character not exposed the bet. Unfortunately for most Americans, those responsible for discovering the "bets" are willfully asleep at the wheel, and Americans have been paying the price for this for more than 40 years.*
>
> *No human being has provided enough labor and intellect in our current economy to be worth $100 million, let alone billions of dollars. That hoarding of capital is on the backs of most working people, directly or indirectly.*

I am sure you have worked for companies and have seen manipulation like the former where advancement had little to do with the person's actual worth. Some are chosen just because …

I am sure you are acquainted with many singers who are on par or better than many megastars. Many artists were "chosen" by the industry. The internet has added some temporary democratization and meritoriousness to the process. But with major corporations controlling the internet plumbing, the corporate structure still has ultimate control.

The sad reality is that the former applies to so many aspects within our economic system.

I further pointed out in the chapter of my book "It's Worth It," titled "Our economic system depends on your path to mediocrity," the following inconvenient truths.

- *Our economic system is not based on pure merit. Instead, it is based on being chosen. In other words, there are many who are qualified, but only a few are chosen. Many MBAs are just as qualified for any job at banks and investment banking firms, but a select few are chosen based on subjective criteria within the qualified group. This applies from profession to profession.*
- *Since the '70s, we have had a 400% productivity increase. In that scenario, we should be working 10 hours a week with abundant leisure time.*
- *The rest of the world was like the heat sink of the internal combustion engine or air conditioner for American capitalism. It afforded a bloated plutocracy, but there was enough for the working class. But to*

sustain the plutocracy's desired growth rates, the American worker became the final source of extraction. As they reach the level of indentured servitude, the entire system collapses.

For us to make a change, we must first understand the pathology of the masters of the economic system under which we live. After understanding it, we can easily see why the masses will never succeed.

If we are to correct our system, it will mean creating a real free enterprise economic system where those who were not chosen or did not want to be chosen can function within an economy where they can succeed because of an established social safety net (Medicare for All, childcare support, affordable education, etc.).

Change starts with getting out of our indoctrination fog. As we continue to tell the inconvenient truths, minds are changed and we will have the tools to assert our worth, demand, and take what we have all worked for.

Chapter 8: Realities of our current economic system.

Over the years I have written scores of essays about the perils of our economic system. In this chapter, I have modified a few of them to make them current. Interestingly, their relevancy to today's economy was astounding. There is still a lot of work to do. The reality is that for too many it has been a continual slide down the economic scale.

I Am A Tough Man but This Made Me Cry and Resolved to Continue Fighting This Class Warfare

I have been mad at our political/economic system for some time. After leaving my activism in college, I settled into a good corporate job as an engineer for 5 years. I then "built" my own software company. While insulated from today's and yesteryears' ills of working for companies that continue wage depression and employee oppression, I read about it with continued trepidation. You see, even when one thinks all is well with where they are in life, the unknowns of society at large invariably will have an effect on us all. As a society we ignore that at our own peril.

On my twitter handle I use the phrase "Political Involvement Should Be a Requirement for Citizenship" because we all make up our own politics. If it is bad, it is our fault. If it is good, it is our fault. After just blogging on political economic issues under several pseudonyms, I decided to just come out and write a book. Hell, everybody on the Right was doing it; mostly distributing factually false information. I was initially wary of coming out publicly because of where I lived, where my daughter went to school, and the potential effect on my business. When I wrote "As I See It: Class Warfare the Only Resort to Right Wing Doom," it was done completely out of frustration and the desire to put the entire operation of our body politic and economic system in a form that everyday folk could understand. The intent was to show how we got where we were, the evils of the current system, and how we get the hell out.

This morning I clicked on a link that got me to a story from a Hostess (makers of Twinkies) employee titled "Inside the Hostess Bakery."[5] I had a visceral reaction to the article because it was the clearest expression of our plutocracy.

It is well reported that Hostess had 6 CEOs in 5 years. It is semi reported that each one had remarkably high salaries and left with big bonuses as they left the company in worse state than when they got there. What is not reported is that the company legally stole employee pensions; monies that the workers contributed. The employees put three dollars for every hour they worked into their pensions. The company borrowed their pensions then went bankrupt. The bankruptcy judge ruled it was a debt they did not have to repay.

Most telling is the terms of the new contract that Hostess wanted employees to accept. The words from the author say it best.

What was this last/best/final offer? You would never know by watching the mainstream media tell the story. So here you go...

- 8% hourly pay cut in year 1 with additional cuts totaling 27% over 5 years. If I, was making $16.12 an hour at the top rate of pay in the bakery. I would drop to $11.26 in 5 years.

- They get to keep our $3+ an hour forever.

- Doubling of weekly insurance premium.

- Lowering of overall quality of insurance plan.

- TOTAL withdrawal from ALL pensions. If you don't have it now, then you never will.

Remember how I said I made $48,000 in 2005 and $34,000 last year? I would make $25,000 in 5 years if I took their offer. It will be hard to replace the job I had, but it will be easy to replace the job they were trying to give me.

This is what the fight is about folks. The titans of finance, the leaders of our plutocracy never have to take cuts. You must remember that the cuts in salaries and benefits on the middle class are related to the plutocracy's increased income and wages. It is a transfer of wealth from the working middle class to the top few. It is legalized theft; sanctioned by our corporate-controlled government.

It is now time that every working, middle class, American take their government back. We must abandon the notion that government is bad. We the people are the government and we the people have allowed the corporate class to take it over by our being gullible and many times willfully ignorant.

Well, reality is staring us all in the face my friends. It is time to band together in groups like Coffee Party USA and Move to Amend and to form coalitions to take the necessary actions to take our country back and force the effecting of policies that ensure us a prosperous middle-class life. The Hostess story is a story that was told, is being told, and will be told if we do not get our act together. How much more of the snake oil policies that continually fail will you continue to support?

Message to The Working Middle Class – Step Up or They Will Step All Over You

From the time you were employed, over 15% of your wages were taken away for Social Security and Medicare. If you were employed by someone else, you paid about 7.5% and your employer paid the other 7.5%. If you are self-employed, you pay it all. Inasmuch as we say the employer pays 7.5% for you, do not be fooled, you paid it because I can guarantee you that absent that 7.5% your salary would be higher. The same is true for health insurance. American wages have been stagnant partially because of increasing health insurance costs. The company forgoes a bigger wage increase because of your health insurance. The employers' cost per employee still increases but the income is transferred to the shareholders of private insurance companies and the providers of inflated health care services and drugs.

I hope you are getting the picture. The cost of everything ultimately is borne by the working middle class. So, this morning after getting back from the gym, I pulled out my Xoom Pad and opened my pulse app. I was shocked by one of the first stories titled "AIG Chief Sees Retirement Age as High as 80 After Crisis." Usually when you read articles like these, you are eased into the reasoning behind the shocking statement. Not this time. The article begins:

> *American International Group Inc. (AIG) Chief Executive Officer Robert Benmosche said Europe's debt crisis shows governments worldwide must accept that people will have to work more years as life expectancies increase.*
>
> *"Retirement ages will have to move to 70, 80 years old," Benmosche, who turned 68 last week, said during a weekend interview at his seaside villa in Dubrovnik, Croatia. "That would make pensions, medical services more affordable. They will keep people working longer and will take that burden off the youth."*
>
> *The crisis, now in its third year, threatens to destroy Europe's 17-nation currency union as Greece contemplates exiting the euro and Spain sees its bond yields rise and banking industry falter. German Chancellor Angela Merkel hardened her opposition to joint debt sharing in the euro region as U.S. President Barack Obama singled out Europe's leaders for not doing enough to arrest the crisis.*

> *Greece abandoning the euro could be a disaster for the country and Europe must work to keep that from happening, said Benmosche, whose company was the world's biggest insurer before it took a U.S. bailout.*

> *"People in Greece have to see there is no easy way out of this" and the government must get them to work longer, he said in the June 2 interview on the Adriatic coast. "If not, and if they go to their own currency, I think they will see huge inflation and it will be devastating for people on fixed incomes."*

Anyone reading this article must conclude that what Mr. Benmosche is saying is that they want workers to work until they die and as such there would be no liability by the state to pay for the promise of a retirement. The man is at his seaside villa in Dubrovnik, Croatia as he is saying this. As I have mentioned in previous blogs, we are so conditioned by the misinformation from our corporate media that selfishness and economic abuse on the working class seem vogue.

I have a message for our working middle class. It is you that made America. It is your labor and intellect that have built the infrastructure and companies of this country. It is you that purchase the products and services you produce whose profits have made the wealthy class wealthy. It is your labor, innovation, and know-how that created the companies that vulture capitalist come into to extract profits with no real risk. As such do not listen to any politician who requests austerity from you. You have been austere for over 32 years. That is how long working middle class wages have been stagnant.

Do not accept any changes in the Social Security promise you had to work for. You must be responsible and understand the game. The working middle class pays Social Security on all their income. The wealthy pays almost none, relative to their share of income and capital gains. Working class Americans must stand on the following principle going forward. We must not accept any changes in our safety net (Medicare, Medicaid, and Social Security) until all income, capital gains and all passive income is taxed the same as the working man's income. It is time for the working middle class to educate ourselves about how changes affect our financial well-being and stand up to ensure it does not continue. It is our responsibility to fight back for ourselves, our families, and our country. The AIGs and other big multinational corporations move from country to county to extract wealth for a select few. As far as they are concerned, the working middle class is nothing but a commodity, an indentured servant that when used up should be discarded at the least cost possible.

Reverse Mortgages – The Final Blow Killing Middle Class Wealth

Many fellow Americans who have worked their entire lives, weathered several recessions and depressions, put their children through school, helped many in need, and faithfully paid their mortgages for decades are being taken advantage of once again. Most have followed all the rules necessary to be considered fiscally responsible, yet because of 'legal fraud' by the financial sector and policies placed into law by purchased politicians, the quality of their retirement years will be compromised.

The Plutocracy, the one percent, has walked away with a large percentage of their 401Ks, their SEPs, and to some extent their financial security. Because of stagnant or falling real wages, much of the working middle class have maxed out on their credit in the attempt to maintain their standard of living. For a Plutocracy that feeds on perpetual growth, from where will it feed now? An old and well-crafted financial instrument known as the reverse mortgage is being marketed on steroids to a baby boomer population.

Before any reader of this article that may have already taken out a reverse mortgage gets upset, please note it is understood that for many this is the only option left. That said, every American should be fighting for a system that allows everyone to build a nest egg that can be transferred to the next generation.

Back in 2010 Senator Fred Thompson was a spokesman for AAG and was pushing their government-backed reverse mortgages. I was writing my book when the commercial came on and I wrote the following in a chapter right then.

> *While taking a short coffee break from writing this book I saw former Republican Senator Fred Thompson, an AAG spokesman hawking reverse mortgages. He says:*
>
> *"Hi folks, I am Fred Thompson. Now like me you probably heard a lot about reverse mortgages but weren't quite sure how they worked or whether they would be the right financial solution for you. Well take my word for it and hundreds of thousands of other Americans who have used the Government Insured reverse mortgage as a safe effective financial tool. If you are 62 year or older and own your own home, give AAG a call and find out how a reverse mortgage can help you. I am extremely*

proud to be associated with AAG, a national reverse mortgage lender that is helping seniors overcome their financial worries and live the lives they've dreamed. Why don't you find out more by calling AAG today? Find out how much call you may qualify for today."

My first thought was how could a former Senator, a senior, a person who likes to tout morality be so callous to entice the elderly to splurge their wealth away. Most Americans have a large portion of their wealth in their homes. Having some wealth to transfer to one's offspring helps the next generation to the next financial level.

Unfortunately, yet another financial instrument designed to use the ignorance of the average American citizen's knowledge of our economic system to donate their money up the wealth tree to the rich. At the end of the reverse mortgage's term, the elderly is left without an asset to transfer to their offspring at the time of their death.

Ironically as this piece was being written Fred Thompson was back on with the 2013 version of his 'working middle class pilfering' commercial.

The most deceptive part of the ad is stating that the owner of the house retains ownership of the home. You cannot own something that you cannot give to someone free and clear. Even more ironic is that Thompson, a professed small government Conservative, is pushing a product that depends on the good faith and capital of the United States government.

Most Americans amass most of their wealth within their homes. Each generation in a responsible family is better off when the previous generation wills their assets forward. Reverse mortgages are yet another financial instrument that stunts the growth of the middle class by encouraging homeowners to extract the capital out of their homes and use it as a supplement to their retirement or to simply splurge. Inasmuch as most reverse mortgages are federally regulated, their upfront costs are extremely high. These costs amount to free cash for the bank and mortgage insurance companies, your money transferred to them for a marginal service.

The big dirty secret is that reverse mortgages, like student loans pre-Obama, are nothing but a no-risk gift to the bankers; a wealth transfer engine from the masses to a select few. When the 'owner' of the home dies, the government pays the bank any difference between the amount owed (interest plus principal) less the sale price of the home. If the heirs want to keep the home, they must pay the loan off in full. If the amount owed is more than the value of the home, the heirs must pay 95% of what is owed to the bank with the government paying the rest. What is the reason for the bank being in the transaction? It is there simply to extract from the government and the homeowner. The bank has absolutely nothing at risk for the profits they make.

Reverse Mortgages mask a systemic problem that affects the American worker; a backward and inhumane retirement system. Every American worker makes a vibrant economy possible by providing 40, 50, or more years of work, taxes, and spending. It is appalling that a worker is incapable of having Social Security capable of providing a decent living. No one should have to deplete all their assets to survive.

The trajectory in this country has been that the wealth and income of the very few at the top grows faster than the growth of the economy. This means that some of that growth is directly coming out of the pockets of the working middle class in the form of lower wages, extractions from the government (tax dollars, interest payments, etc.), reverse mortgages, higher tuitions as states lower taxes, commercial student loans, etc. This is an unsustainable path, and it is leading to a country where the vast majority of citizens will have no assets. They will be functionally indentured servants. They will be nothing but a commodity, a unit of work and service.

Wake up America. Taking this country back from the Plutocracy will require education, resolve, and action. Taking this country back will entail taking back what was stolen through well designed redistribution mechanism that foments a vibrant working middle class.

They only call it Class Warfare when we fight back.

David Cobb, one of the board members of Move to Amend that I served with, sent me the article "Study Busts Myth Corporations use to Justify Skyrocketing CEO Pay" posted on the occupy.com website. To say it got my blood boiling, even as I pretty much presumed the information, would be a mild description of my emotional state after reading and digesting the article and its corroborating information.

There are two premises to the article that I want to put in context.

Executive pay has increased 725% over the last 30 years while worker pay has remained essentially flat.

The second statement is that companies have been escalating executive pay because absent this, the executives would go elsewhere.

I want to debunk the 2nd argument first. The article references the New York Times article "C.E.O.'s and the Pay-'Em-or-Lose-'Em Myth" that pretty much debunks it. That said, common sense alone should have sufficed. There are thousands of MBAs leaving great business schools. Do you think there is a shortage of paper pushers?

Are these executives the real drivers of their industries? Exxon has been in business for decades. Do you think the marginal business knowledge provided by anyone placed in that executive seat is worth the increase in pay they have received over the last 30 years even as their employees, the actual ones that do the work have remained stagnant? The answer is simple. HELL NO.

What we have in America now is a 4-tier class system. We have the poor class. We have the working middle class. We have the professional class. And we have the wealthy class. The wealthy class controls our media and our politicians. They have effectively used both to control the entire country. It is the definition of a growing Plutocracy.

Inasmuch as the wealthy class is exceedingly small, (the top .1%) they have given the professional class the semblance of wealth in that it's worth fighting for by making their lives comfortable and relatively luxurious. We are talking "affordable housing" in exclusive suburbs and/or gated communities, great vacations, company perks, etc., a lifestyle worth defending at all costs. The allure has caused many to compromise their morals.

The working class is busy working. They are busy taking care of their kids the best they can. They do not have much time to do anything else except a periodic vacation. They want life to be better but how? After-all their wages are stagnant, their healthcare is taking a bigger bite, and their children's higher education is taking a bigger bite assuming they can even afford one.

Many in the working class are falling into the poor class even as they are working because of wage stagnation as the cost of a middle-class life continues to increase. These folks get some government assistance, but they see access to the middle class fading.

This dilemma did not occur in a vacuum. It has always been about power. It has always been a small group who wanted power over the many. This was America pre-FDR and is America post-Reagan. While FDR championed a 2nd Bill of Rights that guaranteed the moral existence of a society where everyone was entitled to equal access to succeed, Reagan as the god of supply side economics instituted the effective destruction of a growing middle class as these policies transferred the wealth of the many to the few.

Reagan's famous phrase was the opening salvo on the attack on the middle class when he said, "Government was not the solution but the problem." It was imperative that he unpatriotically disassociate government from the people. Once people no longer saw government as "we the people" the decimation of the fabric of America could begin.

Keeping a policy in effect for more than 30 years, a policy that decimates the masses, is no easy task. It requires a war. It requires a covert and deceptive war. It requires pitting the working middle class against the poor. It demands the professional class be guards at the gates of the Plutocracy.

That is exactly what we have. We have think tanks like the Heritage Foundation and others that can effectively corrupt data to give supply side economic policy the semblance of a policy that works. We have a corporate controlled media that no longer does investigative journalism or research lest they upset the wealthy class that pays the bill. We have the decimation of the unions which is the only body with enough clout, the American worker, to fight against industry and purchased politicians.

We have had class warfare for some time now. Many just did not realize it until now. When I wrote my book "As I See It: Class Warfare The Only Resort To Right Wing Doom," I took a lot of flak for using the term class warfare. I will not back down from that phrase. In fact, until we understand that concept, we will continue our path to indentured servitude with no path to independent success.

Let me be clear. We should not want wasteful government. We should not want a bloated government with a defense budget to protect the world by lining the pockets of the military industrial complex. We should not want a government that encourages a bunch of free loaders. We should not want a government that inhibits free enterprise, the idea that anyone that wants to innovate can do so and profit from doing so. We do not want a government that allows corporations to pollute at will, marginalize workers, and inhibit free enterprise.

Our corporate controlled government is eroding our freedom by design. Corporate control of society has allowed corporations to patent genes and seeds that prevent the little man from innovating and forcing the farmer to buy seeds he once grew for himself. Corporate control has inhibited policies that give the individuals the freedom to leave the corporation and fend for themselves.

Corporate media and corporate politicians push small government for one reason. A small government is a weak government. A weak government means a weak people. Remember government is "we the people." A weak people will be subservient to the new government, the corporation. The only problem is that unlike "we the people" that is the government of the constitution, the corporate government is "we the wealthy few." WAKE UP AMERICA.

Americans are enslaved by the economic system of a dependent wealthy.

Americans are used to being told how to think and what to think. Freedom of choice is cherished yet never really demanded. Americans have allowed the real dependent class, the wealthy, license to enslave.

Those opposed to a truly egalitarian society where government, 'we the people' plays a prominent role in deciding what is best for us all claim that government should not pick winners and losers. They claim the 'free market' is the best arbiter of the most efficient distribution of capital.

What does that even mean? Potholes, medical needs, alimentary needs, shelter needs, and clothing needs exist irrespective of the economic system. If these needs cannot be satisfied within the confines of the economic system, it means the economic system is flawed.

The economic system is manmade. Needs, for the most part, are not. As such it is the economic system that must adapt to a society and not the other way around. Those who practice unfettered capitalism are no different than the ideological clergy who attempt to fit their ancient scripture-driven ideologies into today's realities. The authors of those scriptures likely neither had the tools nor the mental maturity to extrapolate into the future that is now today. But just like many have blind faith and believe in the absoluteness of ancient scriptures, so do those who believe in unfettered capitalism.

Results are all about the effectiveness of the tools. No amount of prayer will change the outcome of one who has Lou Gehrig's disease. No amount of bloviating will change the mathematical certainty that unfettered capitalism destroys the middle-class and provides no pathway for the poor in the aggregate. The mathematics required to illustrate that fact is simple. The narrative necessary to maintain the status quo creates a complexity that gives plausibility to fallacies.

Here are some commonsense realities. The income and wealth of the rich are growing at a faster rate than the economy at large. That means income and wealth must be skimmed from the masses to satisfy that growth. That is exactly what has happened. The manifestation of this is lower wages, outsourced jobs to less expensive job markets, followed by the re-importation of jobs at a reduced wage.

How was this accomplished without notice? Economist/Professor Richard Wolff's "Capitalism Hits the Fan" lays it out perfectly. He showed how Americans were enslaved by the semblance of prosperity pre-2008 Great Recession.

Why didn't the middle-class and poor react as the pilfering was occurring? Detroit activist and Netroots Nation 2014 panelist Maureen Taylor's frog story explains it best. Very gradual changes go virtually unnoticed in the short term but are profound over time.

Now that the profound has occurred and is noticed, why don't the masses revolt? There are several answers.

Salt Lake City Move to Amend performed a skit called "Bread and Circus" that illustrates one component. "There is an old theory of how empires used to control their populous," Ashley Sanders said. "They feed them just enough bread to survive and sedate them with entertainment." Today you get cheap processed food, reality TV, and a plethora of pointless addicting forms of entertainment.

Another component is the manipulation of our actions through manufactured hate. The gays will destroy your marriage. The Muslims will blow you up or cut your head off. The Liberals will give your hard-earned dollars to the lazy Black and Brown people. Liberated women are baby killers. Black and Brown men are to be feared. And on and on. Everyone is fighting each other while keeping their eyes off the real culprit causing them harm.

The most devastating component is the chained American mind. One of the most effective commercials of yesteryear showed a slave liberated from the steel chains. It questions if the mind was also liberated. Unfortunately, if the mind is still enslaved, one is still a slave. That is the new slavery in America. It is no longer slavery not based on race, although race and subclasses are used to feed it. Americans have lost their sense of worth.

Americans have been programmed into believing that capital takes preeminence over humanity. Americans have been programmed to believe that those with capital are entitled to be the arbiters of everyone's success or failure. Americans have been programmed to believe that capital determines one's worth.

Every week on Shark Tank a few capitalists flush with money decide if they will use someone else's idea to increase their fortune. Americans are mesmerized. These guys, generally devoid of scientific training, numerical analysis, and other skills will make one of the beggars rich based on their hunch.

Americans accept that because these capitalists are risking their capital, it is OK to make a fortune that is cumulative based on the knowledge of others while in the aggregate the actual worthy ones get pennies. Americans accept that the risk of the capitalists' fortune is worth more than the risk of the construction worker losing a limb or life. Americans make many other sacrifices of self to ensure the capitalist is comfortable and his risk is virtually risk-free. Donald Trump can be bankrupt one year and in full recovery, two years after, yet middle-class Americans are still unrecovered after 12+ years of crisis and 35+ years of decline.

What is true? The average American is in the driver's seat. Americans with basic skills can live without capital. The average American gives worth to capital, not the other way around. One of these days that light will go off and enough Americans will realize that truth. That is the biggest fear of the wealthy capitalist.

The 47% many of them talk about is a psychological number. In their game, 47% are takers -- almost half. The other 52% are makers.

Those 52% are mad. They are working hard while those loafers take their money. The 52% fight for policies that really benefits the 1% under the false belief that they are sticking it to the 47%. Sadly the 47% that are the 'takers' are just as important in making the economy run like everyone else. They are not takers at all. Their worth is just discounted to create the conflict between the masses to ensure the 1% is not the target as they should be.

The most dependent class in our society is the wealthy class. The masses take care of them. The masses keep their factories producing. The masses invent the technologies that make them profits. The masses buy the goods they sell. And on and on.

To move forward the masses must remove the chains from their minds, discount the lies, educate themselves, and demand what is theirs. They must remove the corrosive nature of money from politics. They must abolish corporate personhood and the tenet that money is speech; likely through a constitutional amendment.

Americans must demand the return of ill-gotten gains resulting from structural defects within our fraudulent economy through taxation. Americans must demand unfettered voting rights. They must demand that all employers pay a living wage. If a business cannot pay a living wage it is not a viable business and just an extender of indentured servitude. Preferential treatment of capital appreciation over working income must end. Social Security taxes must be charged on all income. Health care must be declared a right with basic healthcare paid out of general revenue through taxation of us all. Higher education based on merit must be free. Every working American will pay it forward. A large inheritance tax must be reinstituted to ensure cumulative wealth cannot be extractive of middle-class wealth.

America needs President Biden's middle-class economics on steroids. That is how emancipation begins.

The design of corporations to enrich the few makes them inherently un-trustable.

The design of corporations is a clear and present danger to the well-being of humans.

Recently a friend posted the following prescient phrase by Dr. Joe Dispenza.

> *Warning: When feelings become the means of thinking, or if we cannot think greater than how we feel, we can never change. To change is to think greater than how we feel. To change is to act greater than the familiar feelings of the memorized self.*

The poster posited the question, "Do you lose being authentic in the process. Isn't this strategic thinking?"

I responded stating that living an authentic life is challenging and requires mental fortitude and a thick skin. One must be able to go against the grain even at times at financial and social cost knowing first that you will live proud of decisions irrespective of outcome, and secondly you are playing a part in the outcome you seek. This plays out in political activism, economic activism, and in many forms, others do not see as activism.

IMHO, to be authentic means to always be active in what you believe in. An activist.

The poster segued the thread using corporations as examples. At that point, it gave me an opening to make a much larger point. If we are to change the scourge that the current structure of corporations is to our economy, we must use every one of those offered segues to do so. It is more palatable because it comes from the discussion organically.

The poster made a beautiful statement on getting into the door of corporations' leadership and the executive-level and using that opportunity to onboard others in a more inclusive manner. They believe they could build trust with the corporation to achieve benevolent goals. Unfortunately, that is a utopia anathema to the corporate structure.

The belief that most including middle management are more than widgets in a framework is wishful thinking. Trust and the corporate structure are mutually exclusive as their dominant tenets are:

Whatever the market will bear which equates to total income plus accessible credit.

Fiduciary responsibility is to the shareholders and no one else.

Those corporate business tenets are antiseptic forms of letting you know one cannot be but a cog in the wheel and the deviator will be replaced.

In the upper echelons, to maintain the structure, one needs to know that there are special people to keep this type of system going and that is why there are golden parachutes and other options. One can attempt the fantastical logic of being a part of the corporate structure and with some mutual trust one can build a bigger table to bring others in. That is an unattainable dream designed to placate the conscience of those attempting to justify corporate unfairness with their acquiescence. There are not enough positions for those who want to be chosen to be a part of the corporate structure to give said structure a more equitable existence. Unfortunately, it is just math.

The corporate structure is designed to have an elite, manager class that guards the doors and indentured servants. It has been done effectively for a long time. Progressive policies were there to slow its eventual mathematical collapse or at best drive the acquiescence of the masses to a new form of slavery, one without the whips – own nothing, work, exist, then die.

No one can be sure how Americans will react as the corporate structure destroys healthcare, the environment (very much tied to healthcare with cancer allies, etc.), and everything else. Many Americans are still gullible enough to believe these hazards are our only options. When folks no longer have anything to lose it's either acquiescence or pitchforks.

There are alternatives. It is not enough to be negative. Solutions mean the unearned and undeserved income of those in the corporate structure must be eliminated. Everyone within any given corporation contributes to its success. The wage/salary disparities are responsible for income inequality and wealth disparity.

Of course, the parasites, shareholders, play a big role in being extractive passively. We compensate shareholders for risking their capital. Hell, the workers who inhale the oil fumes or coal dust risk something more valuable to create the income of the rich, their lives. The problem is that we value capital over humanity because we have been indoctrinated that way and it has become our "memorized self."

Corporate executives who really want to make a difference to make a fairer system do no good in helping a few into an immoral structure. They would do well using those huge salaries to help support the activism to correct the system. If they bring in other high-priced executives, make sure they are ones with a moral compass who do not believe they inherently deserve the income differential.

When one's existence is colored by an unfair system that many of us have been a part of for some time, one tries like hell to hold on to it. That is fine. But one should never try to find excuses that do not hold up to math or any other attribute to justify it. It drives activists crazy, especially ones who have given up much to make a fairer system. To be clear, I believe in free enterprise, but that is not what we have in America. Our capitalist market is a man-made creation. It is a verifiable fallacy that capitalism provides the most efficient allocation of resources or assigns value appropriately. Even if that statement were true, shouldn't it matter if the outcome for most people is a steady decline? The fact that a teacher is compensated at a much lesser salary than a stockbroker is probative. After all, teachers move knowledge forward and are ultimately responsible for being the catalyst for whatever the titans of business monetize.

After frustrating the poster about corporations and our current economic system, we had the following exchange.

Poster: I want you to be honest and name aspects of your life where you are benefiting from the offerings of a capitalistic market and what you are doing to rid yourself of those benefits.

My Response: I worked for the corporation for 5 years. I got out because I found it restrictive and unfair. I, along with many, were not rewarded commensurate with what we produced. It always went to the top. That said, I formed a software company and was well rewarded by capitalism. My products were used in just about every major corporation. I practiced real, free enterprise with my company. My values prevented me from doing a few things that would have been more lucrative. Was it wise? At times it seems not. But it does give me the ability to talk more authentically. (e.g., I left $300,000+ on the table during Y2K because my software was implemented correctly making sure that the Y2K rollover was implemented correctly.) It was not that I was so damn smart. While many other companies implemented their software correctly, they still sold new versions. It was their fiduciary responsibility to the shareholder and the market could bear it. When my clients asked if our software was up to date, I simply replied, "You're covered." I have some Boeing and NASA examples I could give as well, but you get the point.

Poster: How do you propose I address your concerns with the hands that feed me? Are you proposing I cut off my nose to spite my face?"

My response: What I wrote was clear. People on the inside can help the movement to make a more equitable system without jeopardizing their employment, just as they did in the Civil Rights movement. The problem is the environment tends to change one. I see too many who throw their hands up in the air and speak that good old phrase, "I GOT MINE!"

Poster: I have done extensive travel in my career and am familiar with the socio-political-economic structure of other countries and must say that the road gladly leads back to the US market structure for me. It's not perfect, but where is? Not even Africa, I want to go back to. I spent a lot of time there."

My Response: I have traveled as well. Moreover, I am from the area the Chicago Boys destroyed. That said, I hear that so often and it is a shallow narrative though it has a semblance of truth. We must understand what empires do. They ensure preeminence by ensuring other systems cannot flourish or succeed. (e.g., when any central American country attempted land management or the elimination of any of the practices that tried to give real free enterprise a chance they were scuttled.) You should not take my statements personally. We are all members and products of the system. That said, one must first operate from facts that are irrefutable. That is why I love numbers. That is the engineer in me. The real question is how we can make a real difference. It is not necessary for all to jeopardize their personal economies though some must and will.

The corporate structure is well designed. Its gatekeepers are found in every sector from think tanks, to media, to schools, to churches and beyond. One should take every given opportunity to get into the part of the gatekeepers' heads that has a modicum of fairness and morality.

Our economic system is designed to keep most people broke by robbing us legally.

A dear friend and Politics Done Right subscriber sent me this meme a few weeks ago. I was appalled but it tells an important story about our economy that every American must understand. It is a bit more complicated and not understanding that it is the reason we accept our continual decline. Please continue reading and share.

Our economic system is designed to rob the masses of all of their income thus preventing the growth of our wealth. We are doomed if we do not fix it.

Our economic system is based on this travesty

MEME: "Humalog insulin, released in 1996, remains unchanged since its release, but the price has increased 1,700% or more since then, from $21 a vial to $375. And Average one year supply (36 vials) has gone from $750 to $13, 500 with zero changes to the insulin."

Gouging Americans for a life-or-death drug has consequences as noted at MedPage Today.

One witness at the hearing, Paul Grant of Gray-New Gloucester, Maine, described the process he went through to get insulin for his 13-year-old son, who has had type 1 diabetes for 4 years. Grant noted that his employer doesn't provide health insurance, so he is paying for it himself through the Affordable Care Act's insurance marketplace, "which is very expensive and very complicated."

With his high-deductible plan, Grant spent $2,500 on diabetes supplies for his son in 2017. He had been paying $300 for a 90-day supply of Humalog. "That seemed like a lot ... until this past January when I called to refill [my son's] Humalog prescription -- it was now going to cost $900 for a 90-day supply ... I kind of went into panic mode," he said. He bought a 30-day supply at Walmart for $322 (with a coupon) until he could figure out a plan.

Grant is now buying the insulin online from a Canadian pharmacy, which charges $295 for a 90-day supply, including shipping. For comparison, last week he looked up the price of a 90-day supply of Humalog at Express Scripts. "It would cost me $1,489 with my insurance."

Jeremy Greene, MD, PhD, professor of medicine at Johns Hopkins University in Baltimore and a practicing physician, has heard similar stories. "Over the past decade in my clinic, when I asked patients why they were not taking the insulin as prescribed, I frequently heard that the cost of insulin is prohibitive," he told the committee. Although Greene first thought maybe he was just prescribing an expensive name-brand insulin instead of a cheaper generic one, "I was surprised to hear that generic insulin simply did not exist."

Instead, three pharmaceutical manufacturers -- sanofi-aventis, Novo Nordisk, and Eli Lilly -- control 99% of the nearly $27 billion global insulin market, even though none of the main agents used are protected by patents, said Greene. "A recent survey found that one of four type 1 diabetics admitted to rationing insulin at least once due to cost in the past year ... Humalog was $21 a vial in 1996 and by 2017, it cost $275 for a 1-month supply ... This has real consequences for Americans living with diabetes."

It is easy to understand why the increasing price of drugs has immediate life or death consequences. What is not immediately apparent is how this mechanism, this economic system by design, is intended to rob you blind.

Insulin is an old medicine, over 100 years old. There is no patent on it. Worse, as noted in the article above, it was virtually placed in the public domain. It should be one of the cheapest drugs on the market but there is a virtual monopoly in companies selling the product. They determine the price. The private sector determines how much they will force you to pay for a drug you must have.

Pricing of any product in our economic system is based on a corrosive concept known as "Whatever the market will bear." And what will the market bear? All of your income plus your total creditworthiness, how much you can borrow.

Sadly, the reality is that corporations whose fiduciary responsibility is to their shareholders and their huge undeserved salaries, will keep raising prices until people are simply unable to afford what they are selling. If it is something they must have, Americans will spend up to their limit to get it.

The tenets of the current economic system are predicated on this behavior that effectively prevents us from saving. It makes us entities that are nothing, but conduits of our income used to create the increasing wealth of a few, those who determine prices, the Plutocrats.

In the past when we made taxes very high on income after a few million, there was no incentive for the legal robbery of the American people through predatory pricing because the ill-gotten gains were recycled right back to "we the people" via taxes.

As politicians on the take reduce and eliminate taxes, the results are clear. Our colleges are more expensive than they should be. Schools are underfunded. Our infrastructure is deteriorating. 80% of Americans are living paycheck to paycheck. But a few people get extremely wealthy, not on their worth or work, but their manipulation of prices, their pricing power.

Is this the life we want? Is this even living? We should learn from these Danish women and work toward a society more like theirs.

The whole sharing economy is a myth.

I was out at the Starbucks in Houston's Montrose area close to KPFT 90.1 FM preparing for my 3:00 PM Politics Done Right show. I had my headset blasting Alessia Cara -- I love that young woman's music --. When I took it off momentarily, I overheard a man talking about driving for Uber and their IPO. Well, you know me. I asked him for an interview. He was not kind to the company.

Mr. Bennett was not just venting. It was also evident that he was not going to allow Uber to hoodwink him. Mr. Bennett understands the concept of real expenses, business models, and much more. Most importantly, he correctly read the tea leaves.

CNBC and other business networks like to sell the gig economy as a panacea for those looking for labor independence, freedom, and economic success. Unfortunately, that model has the same indentured servitude flaw as capitalism.

 The people with the pricing power are not the drivers but the pricing control belongs to the masters who control the software that directs the drivers. They decide who will have the honor to have them command the drivers' pay and indirectly much more.

Mr. Bennett said he used a spreadsheet to accurately reflect his income and expenses (fuel, maintenance, and more). By the time it was all over, he was making less than what he would make on a minimum wage job. He made about $3.00/hour.

That is how the pilfer works. The Gig Economy gives one the semblance of control. The top line payments may seem fine. But what occurs is companies offload much of the expenses that they would typically be responsible for as employee expenses to the individual driver. All of that now comes out of the driver's top line.

Uber knows that as more drivers start figuring out that the business model is exploitative, the drivers will start doing what Mr. Bennett did.

"Uber is working on driver-less cars now," Bennett told me after the interview. "What does that mean for the drivers? They don't care about us."

The Plutocracy continuously sucks all they can get out of workers. They do not want to pay the taxes that will create essential programs like Medicare for All, family-leave, pay-it-forward college, and banker-politician-fraud induced student loan forgiveness, that would make their exploitative model that more bearable.

America is waking up! All we can hope for is that it is not too late.

Chapter 9: Asserting your worth

Americans are taught to believe that they owe something to those who hire them. Ironically, it is mutually beneficial. But understand, our system is designed to ensure that the employee always gets the short end of the stick.

When a company loses money, in the long run you lose your job. But when a company profits, you rarely get a piece of that profit. Remember, profits are wages not paid to you for your labor. It is the perfect skim. We are not taught this because if everyone understood it, our economic paradigm would have to become more democratic. In other words, the company would have to listen to the employees. Unions used to be the enforcers for the employee. As the powers decimated the unions, the workers continued to get less and less of their deserved share.

It is time for the working class to stop accepting crumbs for their labor and innovation. It is time for the working class to demand, not ask, for programs that recover ill-gotten gains from a system that by design penalizes work and glorifies capital.

Scientists research a subject or natural phenomenon in detail. Engineers use the body of work and research done by various scientists to come up with useful products for us all. Doctors in partnership with scientists and engineers develop tools and medicines to provide a service, healing. Businesses employ citizens to sell products and services to citizens. Citizens deposit their savings in banks who lend it out to businesses at fair interest rates that allow the banker and staff a good wage and provides depositors a fair return on their deposits that grow a bit more than inflation.

The above is a simplistic view of what free enterprise should look like. Purposely left out are two specific professions, teachers (from elementary school teachers to university professors) and the movers of capital (investment bankers, corporate raiders, etc.).

Without a doubt, the most important profession in the world is teaching. All the professions listed above were the result of teachers moving knowledge to the next generation. The movers of capital, however, can only be considered a parasitic venture.

The movers of capital have no interest in what a particular business does. The movers of capital are generally oblivious to science and subservient to the dictates of an assumed efficient capital market. Their moves, while making money for a few in the short term, generally hurt those it purports to help. The fact that the movers of capital would support businesses cutting employee hours in lieu of providing healthcare is probative.

The movers of capital lack of wisdom and foresight is evident. Forty years after the oil embargo there were no substantive investments in alternative energy, like what Brazil did. Capital movers have insisted on a business model heavy on outsourcing to maximize profits at the expense of local wages falling and unemployment increasing. Lower wages and higher unemployment are tantamount to lower sales which spiral a country into contraction. This ultimately leads to an eventual and certain depression.

Indoctrinating a large percentage of our citizens into believing that only movers of capital have the wherewithal to create jobs while government cannot, is provably wrong. This is a false tenet that allows many people to believe their unwarranted worth to our society. Small and large businesspeople create jobs. They are worthy of some profits. Government "we the people" creates jobs as well. After –all, teachers, police, firefighters, government scientists, engineers, and the like perform real jobs that add to our economy and societal value. A dollar spent whose genesis is the taxpayer receiving a needed service from the government is no different than a dollar spent whose genesis is a taxpayer receiving a needed product or service from a private company.

Sadly, for the movers of capital, it is imperative that the narrative of 'government not creating jobs' metastasize in the American psyche. Only then can the movers keep unemployment high, wages low, and profits obscene. Is it any wonder they do not want massive infrastructure spending? Too many jobs created will cause wages to go up and profits to be fairer.

The movers of capital have a vested interest in maintaining their façade of worth to society. They must convince us that while the working man pays up to 39.6% in Federal Income Taxes and up to 12.4%+ in Social Security Taxes that they should pay just a maximum of 20% (i.e., all pay 2.9% in Medicare taxes). They must convince our citizens that absent the outsourcing, trading, selling, and bankrupting of companies for which they almost always profit immensely, job creation will continue. The state of the American economy should dispel this myth. The capital movers' goal is never patriotic or noble. It is always to maximize the capital appreciation for a very select few; a privilege most Americans are not privy to.

The reality is that movers of capital have been a detriment to our society. They have used outsourcing and offshoring to keep unemployment high and depress American wages. They have purchased politicians to stop job creation. They have usurped the religious ideologues to further pilfer the middle class. The sonogram laws that were passed in several states over the years create a big market for sonograms. The near elimination of funding for Planned Parenthood will not reduce abortions but instead create a demand for higher cost private abortion clinics. State budgets lower taxes and decimate education budgets as they marginally increase after-tax profits for corporations. Students forced to finance their education with high-cost private loans further enhance the profits for the movers of capital. Implementation of Voter ID ensures that by the time citizens realize their government has pilfered them, the voter suppression laws make them impotent enough to vote the culprits out.

Society has been programmed to deem these characters meritorious of the highest incomes and thus worthy. Worth in America must be reclaimed. Worth must be commensurate with what one produces that provides intrinsic value for the society. This is not at all difficult to ascertain. Absent the teacher, education stalls. Absent the engineer bridges, buildings, & computers are non-existent. Absent the doctors we are unhealed. Absent the scientists we do not have a body of knowledge. Absent the movers of capital life goes on and the local banker who has a real interest in the community is reborn.

Understand this. Capital Markets are no different than casinos. It does not matter that CNBC uses terms you do not understand like collars, shorts, longs, short-squeeze, leverage, EBITDA, and others. These terms are all simple concepts used as gambling tools in the stock market casino.

America's domination by a small class that provides no product or real service to most of our citizens must end. Americans must first visualize and externalize their real worth to society. They must let loose those shackles of indoctrination. The middle class must not accept the current wage or wealth paradigm. The middle class must assert its worth and force politicians to recover the nation's treasure and to invest it in America and Americans who have innovated and done the work to make this country great.

There is a new brand of young politicians asserting their worth. They are empowering others to do the same, by believing.

Why would the 29-year-old Democratic Socialist, Alexandria Ocasio-Cortez, so rattle the Republicans, the Right, and the Democratic Center? The short answer is amazingly simple.

Ocasio-Cortez seemingly out of nowhere:

- Defeated Speaker of the House Nancy Pelosi's presumable successor Joseph Crowley.
- Has a magnetic personality.
- Has a narrative that correlates with the reality of most Americans.
- Won without corporate money.
- Ran a real grassroots campaign.
- Ran on an unabashedly Democratic Socialist platform.
- Built a 2 Million+ Twitter base, which means she can direct a large portion of the national narrative.
- Uses Social Media to get her message out, and counter attacks in real time.

FAIR's Alan MacLeod pointed out an inconvenient truth.

It is impressive how much Ocasio-Cortez has upset the right-wing in such a short time. But when it comes to actual policy issues and not just Twitter spats, it appears the centrist establishment is as uncomfortable with a progressive agenda as the most frothing-at-the-mouth conservatives.

MacLoed also pointed out that many purported Liberal news outlets question Ocasio-Cortezes intelligence and that of her followers. Many sides are attempting to dim her light, discredit her before the fission reaction becomes self-sustaining.

What is the short answer why they fear Alexandria Ocasio-Cortez?

Ocasio-Cortez is a leader in the largest potential voting bloc in the country, the Millennials. Millennials are living the realities that are the effects of all the wrongheaded, greedy and extractive policies of the past.

Millennials see themselves in her. That she lived paycheck to paycheck unable to immediately get an apartment in DC is the reality for many of her peers, any one who've moved back home.

The long answer is even more dangerous. The policies that Ocasio-Cortez promotes puts unfettered capitalism at risk.

Ms. Ocasio-Cortez is beholding to no one. She beat a powerful incumbent who outspent her. Unlike many other politicians, she currently displays no instincts of being ideologically corruptible by those wielding the destructive tenets of the Powell Memo.

That freedom gives her the ability to articulate realities that few are willing to say out loud.

The rich are undeserving of much of their wealth. That is not my envy of the wealthy but instead a moral truth. Amazon's Bezos is worth $160+ Billion. He accumulated wealth on the backs of his employees, some who must get food stamps to survive. Bezos does not have the technological prowess or ability to build the statistical modeling, the intellect that designed the millions of products he sells, nor the labor to move his products. Yet we have an economic system that places him at the top of the reward chain. An economic system is not divine. Its creators bias it towards themselves. At some point, Americans must come to the realization that that arrangement created our wealth disparity and is responsible for everyone's stolen human capital.

An unplugged Ocasio-Cortez will have Americans questioning the why of every part of our economy.

- Why can the individual or corporation profit from natural resources that should belong to us all?
- Why do private banks control we-the-people's money supply?
- Why do we allow profit in the delivery of healthcare?
- Why do we give human rights to artificial persons, corporations?
- Why do we allow pharmaceutical companies to take ownership of drugs invented with our tax dollars and make infinite profits with no recompense to the creators of the drugs, we-the-people?
- Why is income from capital gains taxed at a preferential rate over the working person's income? A rich person may risk "their capital" but human beings risk their bodies, souls, and mental well-being.
- Why is the first question "How will that affect business" whenever one discusses any program of social value while the question "When we go to war?" is never asked?

America's current economic system values capital over humanity. Our mainstream media, the wards of the Plutocracy, are particularly good at keeping the dialogue between the Left and Right rails as many have described in articles pointing out how the establishment plays most Americans.

One can go on and on with questions that show the immoral and draconian nature of our economy that we were indoctrinated into believing serves the common person. Worse, we are made to believe that it is the only way. Our economy serves a few by design. Americans must no longer theorize as to the results and outcome of our system. They are living it. The fairly new and young congresswoman is empathetic. She feels the pain of most Americans who are unwitting victims of this draconian economic system.

While attending a Coffee Party USA board meeting one of our directors said, "You know what makes Ocasio-Cortez dangerous?" She asked and then answered, "She speaks piercingly but civilly. She shows no animosity. She does not come across like a flaming left-wing hack. She just tells it like it is." J'nene Louden, you hit the nail on the head.

Alexandria Ocasio-Cortez is a catalyst that should be feared by the wealth establishment. As our economic disparity widens and as people fall under more economic stress, they will ask these and many other tough questions. The American Plutocracy will not like the answers the other people come out with because it will signal the end of the pilfering. The plutocrats will try to use their "vast legally stolen wealth" to misinform and fool a large enough segment of the population to vote against the popular interests. It behooves all Progressives to get on board and to define the truthful narrative at the grassroots level to inoculate American before we get a further infection.

Chapter 10: Achieving the Utopian society for real.

We were told that man is greedy by instinct. We were told that greed is good. We were also told that greed is the instinct that creates the work ethic that is necessary to excel or to establish excellence.

Those in power have been lying to us from the inception of our economic system. If we were all greedy, then we would never have the plutocrats who sit on money and capital while doing little for it in the aggregate. After all, our collective greed would take it away.

The reality is that most of us are humane. We enjoy coexistence and socialization. Enrichment or the process of getting wealthy does not seem to be pleasurable for most.

There are those who are greedy. There are those who are greedy and selfish. But realize that the pathology is worse. Jeff Bezos could not possibly spend all the money he amassed. Ask the likes of him and Elon Musk if they are willing to immediately rid themselves of their excesses and they will balk.

The bottom line is that most Americans are not greedy. Many have been trained to enforce the rules of our economic system which is based on being greedy and ruthless. Most of us simply play the game for a paycheck to take care of our families and pay our bills.

It does not have to be this way. As I have said ad nauseam. "An economic system is not divine. It is manmade." While it is no longer politically correct to say something is manmade. In this case it is the absolute truth.

So how do we build what would be Utopia for all Americans? Can we build a fair and equitable society? If we want to do it, we can. But it will take two major changes in our mindset. We must first be willing to acknowledge that we are all indoctrinated. Second, we must be willing to educate ourselves from sources who speak truth; sources who can help us break the mental chains.

We cannot have utopia if we do not have the resources. Does America have the natural resources to support its 330 million people? There is no doubt that it does.

America has the natural resources and human capital to establish a near utopian society. The problem is that its economic system is inhumane and has been inhumane from its inception.

When an economic system is based on humanity's worst basic instinct it cannot but create a national cancer. And as the most powerful country in the world, it creates a worldwide cancer.

Does my bottled water story make you want this real economic change now?

We need a massive economic change that in addition to removing power and unearned wealth, identifies and compensates based on one's innate worth thereby ensuring a robust safety net. COVID-19 is bad but here is the opportunity it presents.

I generally work out between maybe midnight and two in the mornings. As I spin and execute my routines, I have been watching Netflix documentaries, learning a lot, getting affirmation for many of my beliefs and much more. It continues to give me a resolve to try to do more. It takes many of us to do it.

Those of us who have the good fortune to vegetate at home unlike the heroes at the hospitals, grocery stores, our garbage collectors, and other hands that truly make our economy work, should consider two very good TV series, "Dirty Money" and "Rotten."

I bring this up because I realize how hard change is from our calculated indoctrination that we have been deceived into accepting as our own. I was having heartburn and my wife brought me bottled water. I immediately felt, like, 'Damn, even my household is a part of the problem.' I wish she had watched "Troubled Water" in the Rotten series.

This is how indoctrination works when we are complicit either by apathy or gullibility to corporate control of our government and our existence.

We allow corporations to take free, available water, to own rights to water, bottle it and resell it to us at prices well more the cost of production and even marketing. Worse, we pay for that water often twice as it is the processed tap water we buy.

It is even more sinister. Corporations promote the neglect of public water infrastructure by creating alliances to depress the tax base (tax cuts, etc.). Sometimes this causes water quality issues. Then they market the bottled water to fix that problem. The thing is that the cost of bottled water way exceeds by orders of magnitude the taxes required to have good water treatment systems available to all. The difference? Corporate executives and shareholders take your money that you could otherwise use to increase your own personal wealth. This is the mechanism our economic system uses to unfairly take your wealth with your consent.

 It gets even worse. All those plastic bottles are now likely living inside of you and your children as the ubiquity of plastic is throughout our ecosystem. Are these multibillion-dollar corporations with their overpaid executives going to pay anything to clean up the mess their "innovation" has created? Hell no. They are already making profits on the remediation of the mess they created.

We are likely going into a depression. The thing is that it will not be widely televised. Maintaining our system requires that we not show its many gross failures. That is why my daughter was in shock when she rode through Appalachia on one of her medical projects. She had never seen poverty like that. It was of a hue seldom acknowledged widely in the mainstream media, that made it more shocking to her. You see, it is essential for one group to believe they are mostly immune to the inherent nature of the extractive economic system we live under.

We are all complicit at some level. What can those who want to do the right thing to make real change do? Many small businesses: specifically, restaurants, hotels, and other places where people go, are gone forever. It is not COVID-19 that is ultimately responsible for their demise. It is a flawed economic system that has no valves to protect society against temporary stasis, a condition caused by unforeseen events no fault of the person proper.

The solution involves redefining corporations by first stripping personhood from them and thus making persons only, persons. This is more complex than most need to understand but it must be done. As such we reserve all rights for real human beings and remove them from some invented entity with unlimited resources. Corporations must have "ZERO" political power. Shareholder value must be the true value of a corporation's assets, period. In other words, the fraud of speculation is eliminated. The fact that there is no mathematical formula for the market means it is a gambling casino. All other concepts are present to allow financial instruments to screw most. We are ultimately always left holding the bag as the dunces-playing-intellectuals of the economic system ultimately fail because it is built on nothing.

The economy is you. They want it to be a controlled-you to take it all from most. If one looks at the charts, there is no question we are heading to complete indentured servitude, serving the 1%, managed by the following 9%.

So again, what can we do? The first thing we must do is forget most of what we have learned about our economic system. Second, we must be willing, to push back on the system and to learn from the many sources objecting to this corrosive indoctrinating system.

A depression is always a fork in the road. The Great Depression introduced social programs to make a better society possible because so many were hurting. It was eroded over the years again through Think Tanks that were used to indoctrinate us.

People are and will be hurting again. COVID-19 survivors are getting their inflated bills. All our health insurance premiums will go sky high because of much higher payouts. Of course, corporate executives and their ilk along with their media broadcasters will not suffer the same pain because the guardians of the gates must be protected to enhance the system's survivability. Hospitals will inflate prices as a result of losing much of their elective business.

The economic change we must demand

Irrespective of who is elected we must demand the following to get the economic change we want:

- Demand Medicare for All,
- Demand student loan forgiveness. This would have been unnecessary or much less if corporations and the wealthy paid their damn taxes to educate the people who ultimately made them rich.
- Demand family-leave.
- Demand massive environmental cleanup to protect our kids.
- Demand subsidized childcare to allow everyone the opportunity to work either for a corporation or themselves.
- Demand rebuilding our infrastructure.
- Demand pay-it-forward tuition-free college.

We can afford all these demands as the economic system is human made and can be redefined to fulfill those necessary human goals. It is not aspiration. Think about it this way. If money is a limiting factor, then we must redefine it to fulfill appropriate requirements in a new economy.

Once again, how do we do this? It is time to organize a national strike after a consortium of groups write the legislation that must be adopted unchanged by those who work for us in Congress. In general, we need an active 3.5% of the population to affect the change most of us want. We must do that and start now.

So, do you see how even bottled water can be, a catalyst for change? What is your catalyst? I am sure there are so many policies we can use to fuse into a change that improves the lives of us all.

Let us keep our eyes on the ball in these difficult times.

I was consumed as I watched the protests. The obvious barbarism of the police's action on a black man, made recounting stories centralized on racism highly effective. Watching others use the opportunity to tell their stories that were visible to all as they spoke to the humanity of many, I said to myself 'KEEP YOUR EYES ON THE BALL.' But let me digress for a minute.

There is a phrase out of the Bible that fits my Humanism. "Do unto others as you would have them do unto you."

What is occurring in the recesses of one's mind that makes them a suspect simply by the skin one is born in ? What is ironic is that the real successful criminal wants to fit in to affect their sport. The irrationality of racism does not even successfully deter. Why? Because it is irrational.

As I am followed around in a store because of my hue, the real shoplifter gets busy. It is funny because criminals who understand the disease, the irrationality of racism, have formed multi-racial crime teams to do just that in many different forms. Hell, Trump is one of the masters, of it. And he is taking all his minions' money in the process.

Similarly, the undocumented person wants to hide and not run the risk of being caught by voting illegally. It is irrational to think that they want to present themselves in a space where they are hunted and could be caught. They just want to work. Most Americans wink because they know the real value of these folks. But for the infected, the semblance of danger and harm from these people allows for effective manipulation.

The powers infect too many with racism, xenophobia, and all the other isms and phobias to divide and control us all by pitting segments of the population against each other. Solving this problem requires intentionality. The government must make laws that mitigate the outcome of racism and all the isms and irrational phobias. But only you can change yourself from the need to be mitigated externally. Absent that, the few will continue to manipulate the many into a steady decline towards indentured servitude.

If we keep our eyes on the ball, we will get through this racial strife and pandemic. We will use it as a catalyst to force a more egalitarian society that will aid in mitigating racism by eliminating certain components that are used as its drivers. COVID-19 will make Medicare for All by any name a requirement. Upcoming natural and unnatural disasters will make us force our politicians to solve our environmental problems.

Let us keep our eyes on the ball. There is much to do. We must enlighten all in a geometric manner.

We cannot allow coerced narratives.

When it comes to politics, it is all about the narrative. Unfortunately, we often fall victim to several forms of messages that put us in a mode where we enter an alternate reality. The culprit: coerced narratives

The Trump administration wanted to oust Venezuelan President Nicolas Maduro. Trump wanted a clean break and the ascension of a new president who represented the Venezuelan plutocracy. To give that America-backed coup legitimacy, Trump, and his allies attempted to create a coercive narrative.

During my interview with Francisco Santos, Colombia's ambassador to the United States, he went out of his way to say that there were 20,000 Cubans in Venezuela, at first implying they were members of the military. When challenged, he clarified that most were doctors and other civilians. He claimed that the operation to oust Nicolas Maduro was led and inspired solely by Latin America. I asked him if Elliot Abrams, Trump's then special envoy to Venezuela, met with the Grupo de Lima, the organization of countries attempting to overthrow Maduro. He acknowledged that both he and the organization met with Abrams.

Santos attempted to push the U.S.-inspired coerced narratives, just as he did in his interview with NPR. It did not go as well. We later analyzed it on Politics Done Right, dedicating an episode to deconstructing it further for our audience. We were not going to be just another outlet allowing the Trump administration to misrepresent facts.

A successful Venezuelan coup would have ultimately served a dual purpose for the Trump administration. Venezuela is a mineral-rich country. He would have held on to several business sectors, because of the expected spoils. Trump also would have gotten a considerable distraction to detract from his domestic legal problems. Trump presented the coerced narrative that America would become Venezuela under a Democratic president.

Roy Eidelson, the author of POLITICAL MIND GAMES: How the 1% Manipulate Our Understanding of What's Happening, What's Right, and What's Possible, recently published an article titled "Stoking Fear: We Must Remember How the Iraq War Was Sold," where he pointed out an important truth: profiteering is the goal.

Despite the devastation wrought, we should not overlook the fact that the Iraq War created its share of winners too. Consider the executives and largest shareholders in companies like Halliburton's former subsidiary Kellogg, Brown, and Root; General Dynamics; Lockheed Martin; and ExxonMobil, to name just a few. These corporations garnered huge war profits through no-bid defense contracts, oil sales, environmental cleanup, infrastructure repair, prison services, and private security. Indeed, speaking to defense contractors at an August 2015 private event, the former president's brother Jeb Bush—who failed to gain the 2016 Republican presidential nomination—explained, "Taking out Saddam Hussein turned out to be a pretty good deal." Notice that they never mention the carnage upon which the war profiteering was built. The lack of humanity on most corporate boards is mind boggling. The antiseptic nature of capital over our brothers, sisters, mothers, fathers, children, relatives, and friends.is what? or is it a septic nature?

Sadly, the high-level machinations that produced the Iraq War are far from unique. History shows that fearmongering has long been a standard tactic used to rally public support and acquiescence for military interventions that are both unwarranted and unwise. It has happened many times before, it has happened since, and it will happen yet again—perhaps soon—unless we collectively learn to recognize, resist, and counter these false appeals from self-serving peddlers of war.

Coerced narratives are very obviously feeding the defense industrial complex. They are used in just about every industry. This was glaringly evident during the Obamacare debate. How could we forget "death panels" and "throwing grandma over the cliff," among many patently false statements.

Even as the Affordable Care Act still came into existence, every profiteer did well at the expense of each American's personal economy.

As we start building the foundation of a genuinely progressive agenda, our American Utopia, we will have to be ready to expose coercive narratives. We cannot expect the mainstream media to be of any assistance. They failed us throughout the Iraq War debate, the Affordable Care Act debate, and many others.

A panelist on MSNBC's Morning Joe initially stated that he would vote for Donald Trump if the wrong Democrat emerged the victor as the party nominee. And of course, there is Chuck Todd throwing shade about capitalism and subliminally calling out Democrats, while Joe Scarborough badgers a Democratic candidate into capitalist submission.

This is an all-hands-on-deck situation. The only way we counteract coercive narratives is by actively engaging on every social media platform. Most importantly, we must support alternative media, from independent sources like OpEdNews.com, DailyKos.com, PoliticsDoneRight.com, CommonDreams.com, and the myriad of other progressive sources.

Employers should pay for employee commute, traffic jams.

Are you tired of traffic jams? Why do we have traffic jams? To put it bluntly, because the only ones who suffer the real cost of traffic jams are the masses. The only people who suffer are the middle-class and the poor. The rich can use helicopters or be driven in fully functional mobile offices.

A few years ago, I got back from Panamá City, Panamá after attending a dear aunt's funeral. I landed in the Tocumen International Airport in Panamá about 3:00 PM. The traffic leaving the airport was horrendous. I had not been in Panamá for 5 years. The traffic has always been bad.

While flying over the city, it was amazing how different the skyline was after just 5 years. I was amazed at my country of birth having a skyline that rivaled Houston, New York, or Shanghai. I wondered who could possibly be living and working in the thousands of units in the center of the city. Did the masses suddenly get large pay increases? Did the masses start getting paid their real worth? Of course not.

As my cousin drove through the traffic jam, I started asking a slew of questions. My cousin is an admeasurer for the Panamá Canal. He determines how much each ship will pay to transit the canal. The amounts are mind boggling. The Canal workers have prized jobs. They get U.S. type wages. However, the masses make very little. Five hundred dollars a month for a secretary is not unheard of.

Canal Workers and some professionals can generally afford to live in or close to Panamá City, most others cannot. They must live many miles away from town. The roads to get into town are congested. Congestion can begin as early as 4:00 AM. Some drivers may spend three hours in their cars trying to travel less than 60 kilometers. Some areas have toll roads. Some of the toll rates would be equivalent to more than half a user's daily income. As such many of these roads are empty, driven mostly by those with nice or luxury cars.

Panamá has a severe case of traffic jams. Throughout the world, including here in the United States, the masses are forced to suffer this condition daily as well. They cause stress. They rob time away from our loved ones. They cheat us of a life that should be much better.

If the cost of systemic traffic jams was placed on those who are ultimately responsible for them, we would have better roads, better public transportation, and better paid employees. How?

When 60 Minutes interviewed Apple's Tim Cook, they covered major corporations keeping their money overseas to avoid U.S. taxes. They spoke about lack of skilled workers in the United States in the same context. What they failed to cover is how successful tax avoidance by corporations and the wealthy are making lives of too many very miserable.

When the wealthy and corporations fail to pay taxes, it cripples education, infrastructure, health care, and much more. And yes, it causes traffic jams.

The masses cannot afford to live close to the employers. They are forced to commute to serve the rich and their employer on their own dime. In other words, the employer implicitly forces them to live far away from their place of employment and the time necessary to go serve that employer is not compensated.

America needs a paradigm shift. Americans need to re-educate ourselves. We have been programmed to be the wards of the state and the corporation. We have been programmed to not notice that in effect, we are indentured servants. We have been programmed to believe the lie that somehow the people that we work for are more deserving of comfort or a rewarding life than we are.

The acceptance of traffic jams as a way of life, the acceptance of poor healthcare as a way of life, the acceptance of poor vacation policies as a way of life, the acceptance of substandard childcare as a way of life, and many other things should never be accepted without a real fight. Many of those who attempt to make things better are maligned because of the indoctrination within an economic system that is progressively failing most of us.

When we fix traffic jams, we will have likely fixed most of our problems. Let us get busy demanding that future utopian society.

American backslide into a vile and overt bigotry

I was not naive enough to believe that America had overcome its intrinsic bigotry as we passed laws to codify equality in employment, equality in education, equality in buying a home, equality in living choices, and equality in most things that affect our external life. Why? Because as people were integrated by opportunity and reality, the fallacies of most of the stereotypes about each other would become moot. Americans would see that basically we all want the same things, we all have the same abilities, and we all have the same faults.

Unity is an extremely dangerous result for a plutocracy. If most people learn the old divisions and delineations were but social constructs to control, then control by the few, control by the puppeteers, control by the plutocracy is lost. When plutocratic control is lost, democracy is born.

Liberals have been demonized because as opposed to seeing enlightenment as a threat to the status quo, they see it as an egalitarian must. If society becomes too egalitarian, the few at the top can no longer hold that pre-eminent position, because society at large would realize that that success was largely built on the backs of the masses. Name any billionaire or millionaire. It is not difficult to prove that his/her success is built on the collective knowledge and work of the masses.

How do you keep a structure where just a few capitalize on the work, service, and intellect of the masses? You infiltrate the media. You infiltrate the educational system. You destroy all organizations attempting to make things better for the masses like unions and cooperatives. You brainwash. You create false realities. You demonize groups. You pit groups against each other. Much of this was detailed in Supreme Court Justice Lewis Powell's infamous Powell Manifesto which was written before he became a Supreme Court justice.

Think tanks designed to mislead like the Heritage Foundation are a reality. The complete takeover of the media especially through outlets like Fox News is a reality. Many Universities have received grants from the likes of the Koch brothers to provide the ability to influence.

All these machinations and deviant behaviors simply delayed the inevitable. America is liberalizing. America is becoming more intelligent. Yes, they may have slowed down progress. However, liberals and progressives continue the slow grind. America is becoming more liberal.

We are now at an inflection point. The plutocracy is fighting back. It however cannot win on reality. It cannot win on policy. After-all, what policy can be offered if the goal is control, if the ultimate goal is to keep a few on top to be served by the masses, the indentured servants protected by a small gatekeeper class, the nine percent?

A backslide into a vile and overt bigotry is the answer. It is easy. It is effective because it revives our reptilian brain. It is the perfect bait and switch technique. It is even more effective when one can use massacres that occur because of policies effected by the plutocracy.

Our daily killings by guns can be directly attributed to policies that flood a market with guns at the same time policies that create a bad economy for many leave many in despair. Islamic terrorism can be directly attributed to our involvement in countries that allow our businesses along with the respective countries' autocrats to pilfer the masses. Does anyone believe Islamic terrorists hate us because they hate our freedom? They hate us because we decided to mess with them. If we left them alone or had actual, equitable relationships they would not care about us.

So, what is a plutocracy to do?

Donald Trump and his ilk demonized Muslims. We used Islamic terrorism to make American Muslims the scary people. They are partially responsible for the defense industrial complex ripping off our hard-earned dollars. Who else is going to mitigate the Muslim problem?

Donald Trump and his ilk further demonized immigrants. They told Americans those immigrants were the cause of them not having jobs or good wages. Of course, the reality is that sending our jobs overseas is the big culprit. It is profitable for the few. And yes, it is the plutocracy that is employing those undocumented workers even as they use them to foment hate.

Not to be outdone, it is common knowledge that existing while black in America is dangerous. The police more so than the general population get good, real-time, target practice as they gun down minorities. Too often they fulfill their disgust and need for personal empowerment by murdering one of a hue too many in the country care too little about. The plutocracy is unconcerned about paying for the lawsuits when irrefutable evidence shows the wrongdoing. After-all it is just a cost of doing business and the cost is spread over ALL taxpayers.

The business of caricaturing some people as more violent and deviant than others ensures the majority think these folks in general are dangerous and we need a police state to keep them under control. And of course, there was now departed Supreme Court Justice Antonin Scalia who ensured that we knew that these lesser people needed to be educated at lesser universities so they could keep up their lesser lives – pun indented.

The plutocracy is on its death bed. Let us remember that we are one people.

When our sun is about to die it will get extremely large. Then the earth will be burned to a crisp. In other words, just like a dying sun can affect irreversible damage before dying, so can a dying plutocracy damage our society. There is a difference. A dying sun follows physics, the laws of nature which are fixed as we know them. We however determine what a dying plutocracy can do. If we engage, we will prevent its death from killing us all.

How do we avert the inevitable Plutocrat driven civil war?

There is a phrase I used to use all the time, "most revert to form." Sadly, we have learned how to live with that corrosive reality. Recent responses to various controversial events and some not so contentious have been disconcerting. The adoration of gaslighting billionaires, inevitable candidates, and more illustrate how we have learned to "revert to form" in our thinking. It has maintained a status quo that will ensure the eventual economic decline for most Americans as a well-paid select few guard the gates that keep most out.

The puppeteers are good. Their planning document, the one very few have heard about, let alone read, laid out the path. And, man, is the Powell Memo working! (You know, the memo written in 1971 by future Supreme Court justice Lewis Powell calling out corporate America.)

When extraction and free labor were needed for just a few to keep the economy going, a brutal form of slavery for "the other," primarily Africans, was adopted at a minimal cost. But the beast needs to be fed exponentially. That means the pool must increase. Guess what? Most in

America were force-welcomed into the new slavery.

External chains and brutality would not work now on the majority. After all, in the primordial stages of this economic system, the pecking order was clear: slavery and the remnants thereof left the majority population with a semblance of having access to success.

Unfortunately, the masses have always been widgets for the plutocracy. Remember, all our laws value capital over humanity. I was on a panel with another businessman on a neutral news program. When I brought up social programs, the first thing the plutocrat asked was how it affected business. Our ruling class never creates social policy first and then adapts the business sector to it. Capital reigns supreme.

The plutocracy will do whatever is necessary to maintain a particular order. Economist and Professor Richard Wolff tweeted a note that hit the nail on the head.

TWEET: "Euro election shows that for capitalism to survive '08 crash & following austerity, it will rely on right-wing nationalism to distract angry workers from the alternative, anti-capitalist left. The compromised old political center is useless. Key question: what will the left do?"

Right-wing nationalism in the United States is serving the same purpose. It could not have occurred without laying the groundwork. It required creating an alternate state of reality that enough would believe.

The Powell Manifesto gave the directions for the plutocracy to infect every institution and aspect of our lives. And with that, it created a new form of indentured servitude. The brutality of slavery was no longer needed. Instead, the chains are now mental, and people absorb them at different ideological levels, from the extreme to the mild.

The difficulty is keeping the different poles that comprise the masses balanced. They must be preoccupied with one another and not with that which is inflicting pain and bleeding them dry.

The plutocracy depends on polarization, and so far, it has been successful. Trump was not the genius of the plutocracy. He just magnified the hate at the appropriate time. He was only the puppet of the system which chooses its protagonists not only in America but throughout the world.

How can likely the most corrupt president continue to hold on to near-unanimous Republican Party support and maintain a Democratic establishment at bay? Could it be that until an acceptable Democrat is on a glide path he is kept whole?

The plutocracy does not seem to realize how profound the manufactured hate is between the poles. And they are well armed. A caller to my show Politics Done Right recently illustrated the level of seeded irrationality as he pointed out that Trump could do nothing wrong that would worry them.

A civil war?

How close are we to a civil war? I think we are closer than many people think. How do we avert it?

Averting any form of a civil war requires breaking mental chains. We must step out of our comfort zones. Many continue to revert to form even as they start to see the con because it is more comfortable mentally, and to some economically as well. But the big picture down the road for most will be dire.

Those doing the kind of work we are doing, progressive activists, must stay the course and do the work of not allowing the forces we know are working to undermine us all to go unchallenged. It is existential. Never give up. The spears hurt less when you know you are doing the right thing.

All systems that hurt their masses will ultimately fail.

To "Democratic Socialism" or not to "Democratic Socialism" is the question.

Many rebelled when Republicans made liberal a pejorative. How dear they force us to deny who we are? The "Democratic Socialism" moniker best defines the policies many progressives support. As such, they had no problem supporting the Democratic Socialists of America (DSA). But maybe for election cycles, we need to be a bit more strategic.

Americans have been programmed to believe that capitalism is the best economic system. They have been conned into believing it somehow correlates with democracy. Neither is true. In fact, by design and definition, capitalism can be inhumane. China is both a communist and a capitalist country.

Capitalism is defined as "the invisible hand of the market," "the efficient allocation of [scarce] resources." Efficiency is not always humane. In a system where the fiduciary responsibility of those running the basic unit of the capitalist economic model, the corporation, is to the shareholder. The effects on humanity are far-reaching and immediately evident by today's reality.

There is nothing democratic about capitalism. Nor does it need to exist within a democracy. As the plutocracy disenfranchises unions, there is a master-servant relationship between employee and corporation (executives & managers).

When the class who owns the most capital can get wealthier at a faster clip than those who do not, it becomes a classic example of not only capitalism's inhumanity but also its immorality. Think about it.

The folks who invest capital in building a skyscraper are entitled to a return in perpetuity for that investment while they pay worker-capital once.

Both the investor and the worker use a form of capital. A wealth driven class gives the work-capital, read human-capital, less value. But that is not all.

The appreciation of capital, a form of income, is taxed at a lower rate than the person who works. While some would say that the taxing laws are not part of the capitalist economic model, that is hogwash because the practical operation of the system in the aggregate is what matters including the corrosive nature of the wealthy bribing politicians to get their way.

This particular story, the insulin story, is a perfect example of the corrosive and irreversible nature of capitalism through those who control pricing power. Pharmaceutical corporations raised the price of insulin, a product the taxpayer paid for by several hundred percentage points. It is the type of behavior that governs our economic system

> *Ultimately, those with unregulated and unlimited pricing power on products and services you must have, can ensure one can never accumulate wealth. They own you. They can extort from you.*
>
> *The above reality defines our economy. And the proof is a continual decline in the wealth of the masses as the few gets a more significant percentage. Unchanged, math prevails. Welcome to indentured servitude.*

Until Progressives find the narrative to deprogram those who think our system is democratic or divine as opposed to human-made to enrich the few, change will not happen.

And then there is Democratic Socialism -- the word too many people fear. I wrote a recent article for the Daily Kos titled, "Want the GOP to stop using the word 'socialist' to scare off

Democrats? Make 'capitalism' a bad word" a few months ago.

> *I believe in having an economic system that works for everyone. It must be Democratic. The best one is a hybrid featuring free enterprise and a robust safety net, a system unable to hoard capital, which is a detriment to the economy.*
>
> *Everyone should have the ability to create their own company if they so desire, using their intellect and labor to get compensation commensurate with their efforts. Many who read some of my anti-corporate/anti-capitalist rants likely believe that I am a blowhard who wants a socialist state, where the takers abuse the makers. That is not so. What is clear is that the food stamp con artists share much in common with most of the unfettered capitalists: They are takers by design -- they both profit from the labor and intellect of others (e.g., taxpayers and employees).*

Disagreeing with the snippet above is hard. And in fact, it is entirely in line with the tenets of Democratic Socialism as laid out by the DSA.

Democratic socialists do not want to create an all-powerful government bureaucracy. But we do not want big corporate bureaucracies to control our society either. Rather, we believe that social and economic decisions should be made by those whom they most affect.

Today, corporate executives who answer only to themselves and a few wealthy stockholders make basic economic decisions affecting millions of people. Resources are used to make money for capitalists rather than to meet human needs. We believe that the workers and consumers who are affected by economic institutions should own and control them.

Social ownership could take many forms, such as worker-owned cooperatives or publicly owned enterprises managed by workers and consumer representatives. Democratic socialists favor as much decentralization as possible. While the large concentrations of capital in industries such as energy and steel may necessitate some form of state ownership, many consumer-goods industries might be best run as cooperatives.

> *Democratic socialists have long rejected the belief that the whole economy should be centrally planned. While we believe that democratic planning can shape major social investments like mass transit, housing, and energy, market mechanisms are needed to determine the demand for many consumer goods.*

If anyone believes this is pie in the sky, consider the Mondragon Corporation, a Spain cooperative. In 2015 it employed north of 74,000 people.

These are two economic cases laid out very superficially but are very understandable. Polls tell us that policies that would democratize the economy is what Americans want.

After the indoctrination and the vilification of certain words for generations, Americans will not just make a change on faith. They have no examples of Democratic Socialism working anywhere. The Plutocrats and many in our government, Democrats and Republicans alike, go out of their way to defend the pilfering status quo by equating the social democratic economic model with all the places where some false variant failed while hiding in plain sight the parts of the world where some versions are working.

Elizabeth Warren upset many when she stated she was a capitalist but with a whole lot of controls. One should gain a much better appreciation for what she is doing. It starts with the Accountable Capitalism Act.

- Requires very large American corporations to obtain a federal charter as a "United States corporation," which obligates company directors to consider the interests of all corporate stakeholders.
- Empowers workers at United States corporations to elect at least 40% of board members.
- Restricts the sales of company shares by the directors and officers of United States corporations.
- Prohibits United States corporations from making any political expenditures without the approval of 75% of its directors and shareholders.
- Permits the federal government to revoke the charter of a United States corporation if the company has engaged in repeated and egregious illegal conduct.

Remember the Bush's Clear Skies Initiative? The name made one believe it would be an environmental panacea -- clear skies, smog-less skies. It was the narrative that most people absorbed.

To "Democratic Socialism" or not to "Democratic Socialism" is the question. Elizabeth Warren knows how best to answer it. Going forward until we invest enough in reeducation and the eradication of fallacies, we should make the policies speak for themselves -- no labels required.

There is absolutely no doubt that we can pay for Medicare for All and we better!

I was the speaker at a Democratic Club that meets in a very Red area in Houston Texas. Many of the members are centrists. My goal was to illustrate to them why centrism will not win 2020. What better way to illustrate that than with Medicare for All?

It is important that we manage ourselves into Medicare for All or we will parachute in with equipment failure. Increasing health care prices at a rate faster than inflation and wage growth is unsustainable. Companies will milk the gravy train until they can no more. It would be ironic if the switch occurred under a Republican.

One of the attendees told me that while they support Medicare For All, her priority was to remove Donald Trump and as such is a centrist. Her belief is that centrist policies would win the White House. Unfortunately, that has coalesced to a well-designed false narrative.

Sitting in that room were a couple of millennials high up in the party. Interestingly, they agreed that given their condition- no health care, high student debt a centrist position is no different than a Trump position. The difference between poverty and abject poverty is not worth the effort to reward any party that cares little about their future; one that is immoral, the other timid.

Polls already made it clear that Americans want Medicare for All and other Progressive policies. The only way to win on a centrist agenda is to pull those numbers down.

The plutocrats were using two arguments against Medicare for All. The first was that it would cost so much that taxes would go up. The second is that you will lose your private insurance. Both statements were true with some very important caveats.

In short, taxes would go up but payment for health insurance premiums would be eliminated and every American would have medical coverage from birth to death. One would be left with more money in their pockets because in addition to no insurance premiums there would be no deductibles, co-pays, in and out of network costs etc.

The original idea is to get rid of health insurance companies. They do not provide healthcare; they restrict healthcare to make passive shareholders a profit and overpaid executives an undeserved large salary and bonuses.

We can pay for healthcare with more equitable taxation. Currently, every American indirectly through rent or directly from owning a home and/or a car pays wealth taxes. Our wealth takes various forms, real estate property, stocks, bonds, etc. A small percentage of Americans own most of the wealth in this country.

The rich get a huge implicit welfare check because their assets are held in forms, they have paid politicians to keep untaxed or undertaxed. That is yet another reason why the wealth disparity is ever expanding. They get preferential treatment as they extract more from everyone.

For those who believe it is about wealth envy, one would have to first have a modicum of respect for the way the super wealthy amassed their fortune. Anyone who wishes to understand real economics and not what they teach in business schools would immediately understand that the wealth of most of the super-rich is made on the backs of others.

Their wealth is the money they decided not to pay their employees or those working for them to accumulate said riches. For that reason, it should be taxed at a higher rate than the common person's earned wages. Unearned capital gains and income does not warrant preferential tax treatment.

Is the money to pay for expanding Medicare to cover everyone there? Yes, and a lot more to do all of the things we need to do to fix infrastructure, education, and more.

There are two important stories that one must watch. The first is that H.R. 676, the number assigned for Medicare for All every year, is no longer. The new bill is H.R. 1384, the Medicare for All Act. The second is that during the development of the bill, a Nancy Pelosi aide told insurance executives not to worry about Democrats pushing "Medicare for All."

Here is a warning from this activist in the field. Millennials are the largest voting bloc in the country. A large percentage of them are in dire straits. The country has the money to give us all health care if we do the right thing, stop welfare for the rich. When people feel like they have nothing to lose they don't vote, or they penalize. Millennials will not accept another betrayal in the subsequent years.

A 22-year-old kid gave this old activist a boost and faith in the youth.

I was sitting in my 2nd office, Starbucks, packaging my book As I See It: Class Warfare The Only Resort To Right Wing Doom at my website which allows subscribers to read it online (a well-intentioned gimmick to help support Politics Done Right). And yes, I intend to continue supporting my local Starbucks and other coffee shops irrespective of Howard Schultz' fall from progressive grace. Activists are working to recover what billionaires and the wealthy legally extorted from us.

Anyhow, I posted the following on my personal Facebook page that generated some great civil discussions.

> A 22-year-old Kingwood kid just made my day, and he likely does not even know the boost he gave me.

> I was sitting at the table blogging at Starbucks when a regular comes up to ask me the daily question. He asks me what I am blogging about. I told him I am posting a blog from a guy I recently interviewed about capitalism vs socialism. The patron said, "Count me out of that democratic

socialism thing. I like capitalism." This guy is on social security and Medicaid. I asked him if he likes Social Security, Medicare, and roads. "Of course," he replied. I asked him if he would like them to be better. He said he did. I told him that he likely is just like me. He said no and walked off.

I could see the young man across from me listening attentively. I asked him what he thought. At first, he did not want to get into it. I figured (why one should not assume), a Kingwood kid, he is going to start the standard prose. Well, he did but not one I would have expected.

He said rightfully there are flaws in all systems. But he acknowledged how bad our economic system has become for the average person. He served the country for 3 1/2 years right out of Kingwood High. His healthcare ended the day he stepped out of the military. He gets help for 3 years of college then he is on his own. He is forced to buy books he will not use to satisfy the book corporations who own the politicians. ("$350 for a book I will never use," he said. He then started talking about inclusivity and that many of the old people just are not getting why.

Why was this exciting? He told me all of this without me coaxing any of it out of him. The young people are getting it. They are seeing how much we have screwed them.

We better get it right for them while we have time to atone for the individualistic selfish people many of us became when Ronald Reagan made it vogue.

That kid makes the activism many are doing well wort I am doing well worth it as difficult as this shit is. That was the most rewarding engagement I had in a long time.

It is important that activists realize much of what we are fighting for will not be realized for decades. That is why it is important to connect with those who will accrue most of the benefit.

She cried. She finally got it. Like hers, the lives of many are at risk without healthcare.

"Egberto, get this woman on your show," was the screaming Facebook tag I got from Daniel Cohen, my good friend, and President of Indivisible Houston. I immediately read her message, and my heart sank. I was happy for her, but have we come to this? Really?

Here is the Facebook post from our friend Stephanie Person, a community organizer in New York.

> *After TWO YEARS without healthcare, I came home to see that I finally got my insurance ID card in the mail. First, I was silent. Then, I cried happy tears.*
>
> *I feel a huge sense of relief. A weight released that I did not know I was carrying around with me. For the past two years, I was working as a contract worker, which means I was not entitled to health insurance through my job.*
>
> *Whenever I got sick, I would just ignore the problem until it went away. I have not been to a doctor in over TWO YEARS*

because I never knew how much I'd end up spending out of pocket.

I am lucky that chapter is over for me, and I'm lucky that I've been in good health, but many are still living without healthcare coverage. Many have the added stress of preexisting conditions, special needs children, and expensive hospital bills. Even the simplest procedure can cost thousands of dollars.

Many are poor, but not "poor enough" for Medicaid (in 2018, the threshold was $28,676 per year for a family of three and $16,753 per year for an individual).

75% of Americans are living paycheck-to-paycheck, which means unexpected surgeries are out of the question for those who are uninsured. For many of us, the healthcare "plan" is getting rushed to the ER when it's often too late.

Though so many of us struggle, we are a wealthy country—we should not have people dying because they did not crowdfund enough for life-saving surgery. Other countries with far smaller economies can take care of their citizens—why can't we?

> *There is no real reason except greed. Therefore, we shouldn't be tying healthcare to people's employment. Therefore, we need a #singlepayer system. Therefore, we need #MedicareForAll.*

These are the words of one young woman who was ecstatic that she got something that should be her birthright. She got healthcare.

I was invited to speak at the weekly Indivisible TX-02 Northeast Houston meeting then. One of their leaders, Patricia Day Gallini, asked me to speak about the Politics Done Right show about a doctor who so feared the word "Socialism" that he would rather be a corporate slave. He used the word slave when he described how hard he must work because of what the executives are doing to cost save -- read, maximize profits for the execs and shareholders.

When doctors are young, millennial woman and doctors are both victims of a system, it is clear the current system should not exist.

Social Security & Medicare easy to fix requiring no cuts. GOP WRONG!

Republicans early in the Trump administration passed a huge tax cut that can only be defined as a tax cut scam that transferred yet again your hard-earned dollars to a wealthy few. After the deficit began exploding because of their fiscal irresponsibility and conniving posture, Republicans wanted to balance the budget on the back of the poor and middle-class. The solution? Cut Social Security and Medicare.

It is not at all difficult to make these two programs solvent. Robert Reich details how in his article "Three Easy Fixes to Social Security and Medicare that Republicans Don't Want You to Know About."

> *First: Raise the cap on income subject to Social Security payroll taxes.*
>
> *This year, that cap is $128,400, meaning that every dollar earned above $128,400 isn't subject to Social Security taxes.*
>
> *So the typical CEO of a big company, who makes over $15 million, pays Social Security taxes on just $128,400 of his or her income, a tiny fraction. While the typical nurse practitioner, who takes*

home around $100,000, pays Social Security taxes on every dollar of his or her income.

In this era of raging inequality, that's not fair. And it's not even logical. Raise the cap.

The reality is we should not just raise the cap. We need to get rid of the cap and make it completely progressive. That would likely allow us to lower the rate itself which currently stands at 12.4% for Social Security and 2.9% for Medicare.

Second: To help rein in Medicare costs, allow the government to use its huge bargaining power to negotiate lower drug prices.

Big Pharma has gotten legislation barring the government from negotiating lower drug prices. That legislation should be repealed.

Big Pharma says this would mean less research on new drugs, but that's baloney. Pharma already spends more on advertising, marketing, and lobbying than it does on research.

Negotiating drug prices is a start. Additionally, all drugs that were developed with government grants, likely most, should profit share with the government commensurate with the government's, we the people's, investment.

Third: To deal with a basic reason why Social Security and Medicare are running out of money, allow more young immigrants into the U.S.

The basic reason why Social Security and Medicare are running out of money is the American population continues to age and live longer – leaving a relatively smaller working population to pay into Social Security and Medicare.

What to do? Allow in more young immigrants. Immigrants and their children are the fastest growing segment of the working population, already contributing billions in payroll taxes every year. Instead of shutting immigrants out, allowing more immigrants into the country will help secure the future of Social Security and Medicare.

This is not rocket science, folks. Raise the cap, negotiate drug prices, and allow in more immigrants. Do these three things and you will not have to worry about Social Security and Medicare not being there when you need it.

When a friend of mine, a Trump voter, realized that immigrants will allow him to retire without a Social Security crisis, he found an ideological way to support a comprehensive immigration policy. He wrote a post which I think could start an immigration dialogue between the Right and the Left.

Do not buy the continued Republican lies about jobs or having to cut the social safety net, Social Security and Medicare. They represent us and not just the wealthy who benefitted from the good labor of all Americans.

Only a Progressive renaissance can rebuild the middle-class.

The last time our country was governable was in 2009 and 2010. Democrats had a supermajority in the Senate and a substantial lead in the House of Representatives. During those two years, President Obama got more accomplished than any president since FDR. In fact, the policies passed during those two years are responsible for all economic progress, however anemic, under President Obama.

President Obama was unable to enact any substantial policies after that. Why? -- because Republicans took over the House and subsequently the Senate. Gridlock is dysfunctional.

Republicans had an agenda based on the debunked tenets of austerity exposed by a 28-year-old grad student. An Ayn Randian sect who did not mind lying to their constituents in their attempt to pass policies beneficial solely to their wealthy benefactors led them. In doing so, Republicans ensured an economy that grew at the slowest rate of any recovery since WWII. Of course, it is also the longest sustained recovery ever. Even so, most Americans are not partaking of this continued economic growth.

Americans, especially millennials are fed up with political parties. When Democrats had their supermajority, they had the ability to pass legislation in a manner that would have insulated them from Republican misinformation.

In 2009, the healthcare fight was not between Republicans and Democrats. It was between Progressive Democrats and Corporatist Establishment Democrats.

Had all Democrats worked in the interest of the middle-class and the poor by using their once-in-a-generation political power to pass the only mathematically plausible and affordable health care program, single-payer Medicare for All, Americans would never vote for the false promises of a market-based health insurance again.

Had all Democrats told the truth, that taxpayer dollars are responsible for most of the R&D for drugs later marketed by pharmaceutical companies at obscenely escalated prices, it would have made it possible to curtail pricing and forced pharmaceutical companies to share their unearned windfall profits with the Treasury. That would have been the fair thing to do.

Had Democrats instituted pay-it-forward tuition-free college, they would have owned the young vote. Had Democrats established a national daycare plan that allowed all who wanted to work the opportunity to do so, they would have possessed the votes of those who wanted children.

One could go on and on. Just if. These are all benefits that poll over 50% irrespective of party or ideology. Of course, these policies will not garner support from those extracting their unfair share of wealth from the excess labor of the vast majority of Americans. They would have Americans believe that they are begging for free stuff. They are takers.

Here is the reality, those who reap excess profits at the expense of a society that is humane are in fact the takers. Their excess profits are your income and wealth deficits.

Our learning institutions do not teach basic courses in economics that allow them the ability to discern the real reasons for the collapse of the middle-class as the masses march on to virtual indentured servitude. Our schools no longer teach civics. Why? -- because an informed population would not donate their labor and intellect in a manner that only benefits their employer, the wealthy, the few.

As we enacted progressive policies in the sixties and seventies, the American plutocracy had to act to arrest the enlightenment of the masses. That action came in the form of the Powell Manifesto. That single document was the road map to institutions of misinformation and the dumbing down of America.

But one should not despair. The stars are aligning for the Progressive renaissance. We all knew that Donald Trump was lying to his followers. He commands a shrinking base that operates in panic mode as a vocal and seditious opposition.

The goal of our plutocracy is not to satisfy the masses. Their intent is to restructure government to allow a permanent governing minority. Gerrymandering, voter suppression laws, and a friendly judiciary are their building blocks for their new form of governing.

It is not a reality yet. The remnants of the Trump cabal is not making it any easier. Progressives do not have much time. The time is now.

Americans know their political system is in shambles. Enough took a chance on Trump. I must digress here.

Many want to put Trump's win on Russia. If Russia did not hack voter machines, everything Russia did to help Trump win, could have been done by Trump with the money he would have had available to him.

Hillary Clinton spent much more per vote than did Trump in the aggregate. The problem is evident. Democrats simply lost the support of too many voters even though they had a platform backed by most Americans.

Several Progressive organizations got involved. Some are teaching civic engagement. Some are policy specific (e.g., Physicians for a National Health Program). Some are even running candidates (e.g., Brand New Congress, Our Revolution, People's House Project).

Just like today's doctors attack viruses with several different medicines at once to prevent mutations from rendering drug therapies ineffective, so must Progressives attack the virus that is the resulting effect of the Powell Manifesto.

The stars are aligning. If Progressives do not take hold now, they are unlikely to get another opportunity before some revolution sets in as the despair of the masses multiplies.

All peace-loving Progressives must activate. The country is at the tipping point.

On what side will we tip? The masses have only two choices, the continued march to indentured servitude or the building of the American Utopia.

So how do we get to our Utopia?

The previous chapters explored our current realities. We touched on economic systems. We discussed how the system holds us hostage via indoctrination and other techniques.

We made the case that our multi-millionaires and billionaires are enriching themselves with our excess labor. In other words, their wealth comes from wages directly or indirectly denied those that do the real work. Simplified, if a car cost $5,000 to build and they sell it for $15,000, shareholders and executives pocket the $10,000. They could not have made that without the worker. Under our current economic system for the most part, you do not get to share in the fruits of what you produce, your excess labor is legally stolen.

Sadly, we made an important case that is hard to swallow. The form of capitalism under which we live created a new kind of slave, one that requires no chains as they are now virtual. We are now members of a new kind of slavery, antiseptic slavery.

Too many of us have adapted to and accepted our current condition. Why? We are either made to feel impotent or we are so indoctrinated that we believe this is all we have got. Ironically, we feel impotent because we are embarrassed to believe our reality. "Only those others could be in a state of permanent subservience." So, we put our heads in the sand and just go through the motions. We exist. We do the best we think we can.

Creating our American Utopia is a long-term project. It requires a paradigm shift and new ways of thinking. I have alluded to many of these in the previous chapters.

How do we even start? I see it as a two-stage process. Stage 1 involves preventing us from falling into some form of fascism. Show that a democracy can take care of its people. Do not allow the "good" to be the enemy of the "less-than-optimal."

Elect the best candidates whether progressive or somewhat less than progressive. Work with them to get specific changes to make the lives of the most needy, bearable.

The first phase of this transformation has already begun. In 2020, a grand coalition of many who would not normally work together did just that. In the process they saved the country from a precipitous fall into fascism.

As we shore up the country, we must start working concurrently on Phase 2. What does that entail?

Phase 2 requires engagement with the entire electorate about the advantages of an egalitarian system. We can use many of the examples we discussed in earlier chapters to make it clear that the current economic system is not only immoral, unfair, and selfish, but unsustainable. We must change the belief of most that the current system values them. Most importantly as stated in some of the earlier chapters, the economic system is not divine. It is manmade and must change.

Americans are not opposed to these concepts. They just need to be informed about them in a civil, respectful, nonconfrontational manner.

How do we reach all the people we need to reach? The answer is simple – by, all means necessary. Whether you are in the grocery store, the pharmacy, the coffee shop, a department store, bakery or anywhere else, do a lot of listening and either start or join a conversation in a manner that opens the door for lasting dialog.

But we all must do more. Our corporate media is funded by many of the same corporations that oppress. With the advent of the internet, hundreds of independent media organizations of every stripe are online informing and organizing. Support them both financially and by sharing their blogs, articles, tweets, newspaper articles, radio/media shows and everything in between. Personally, I support DailyKos.com, OpEdNews.com, CommonDreams.com, DemocraticUnderground.com, and several others. And of course, I support our own, PoliticsDoneRight.com.

You can start building the American Utopia here

I want us all to remember that there is nothing more powerful than an engaged we-the-people. As an unabashed optimist who believes that eventually our empowering message will be disseminated broadly and effectively, I decided to do my part by:

- Hosting/producing the radio show "Politics Done Right" that is available at KPFT 90.1 FM Houston, a Pacifica Network station as well as on the internet at politicsdoneright.com every weekday.
- Posting blogs that amplify, expand, expose, or inform on current news or on "hidden news" from my site egbertowillies.com several times a day.
- Creating informational / educational / political videos at our YouTube channel at youtube.com/egbertowillies several times a day.

- Writing information & empowering books.
    - o As I See It: Class Warfare The Only Resort to Right Wing Doom.
    - o It's Worth It: How To Talk To Your Right Wing Relatives, Friends, and Neighbors.
    - o How To Make America Utopia: Take away the economy from those who rigged it

Become a part of the Politics Done Right Posse affectionately known as the PDR Posse.

We are building an informational posse to go along with this book. All resources are posted at politicsdoneright.com/pdrposse for your easy access.

Our posse is fun. Even as I am ideologically progressive, our posse includes people of all ideologies and every day we have healthy discussions during and after the daily Politics Done Right show.

Let us be a part of changing America for the better tomorrow. Let us help create the American Utopia.

politicsdoneright.com/pdrposse

Notes and Links

http://www.pbs.org/wnet/supremecourt/personality/sources_document13.html A memorandum written by Lewis F. Powell Jr. in 1971 to Eugene Snyder at the U.S. Chamber of Commerce.

 E. Willes, https://www.chron.com/neighborhood/atascocita/opinion/article/Middle-class-held-hostage-9379785.php

P. Brown, D. Lee, K. Sopoci-Belknap and E. Willes, https://egbertowillies.com/2013/10/18/legalize-democracy/

Tables and references to the U.S. Economy, https://en.wikipedia.org/wiki/Economy_of_the_United_States

D. Hope, https://www.chron.com/life/health/article/Jesus-is-not-a-socialist-9370988.php

E. Willes, https://egbertowillies.com/2019/02/13/greedy-plutocrats-takers/

Elon Musk's 2018 tweet https://egbertowillies.com/2018/08/08/tesla-elon-musk-stock-economy-fraud/

60 Minutes Tim Cook interview in 2015,
https://www.cbsnews.com/video/apples-tim-cook-talks-tech-and-privacy-with-60-minutes/

R. Wolff tweet on Euro election,
https://twitter.com/profwolff/status/1133418908382142465?lang=en

All the current bills including H.R. 1384 are posted in www.congress.gov/bill